Opera
A Beginner's Guide

ONEWORLD BEGINNER'S GUIDES combine an original, inventive, and engaging approach with expert analysis on subjects ranging from art and history to religion and politics, and everything in between. Innovative and affordable, books in the series are perfect for anyone curious about the way the world works and the big ideas of our time.

anarchism	forensic science
aquinas	french revolution
artificial intelligence	history of science
the beat generation	humanism
biodiversity	islamic philosophy
bioterror & biowarfare	journalism
the brain	lacan
the buddha	life in the universe
censorship	literary theory
christianity	machiavelli
civil liberties	magic
classical music	mafia & organized crime
climate change	marx
cloning	medieval philosophy
cold war	middle east
conservation	NATO
crimes against humanity	the northern ireland conflict
criminal psychology	oil
critical thinking	opera
daoism	the palestine–israeli conflict
democracy	philosophy of mind
dyslexia	philosophy of religion
energy	philosophy of science
engineering	postmodernism
the enlightenment	psychology
epistemology	quantum physics
evolution	the qur'an
evolutionary psychology	racism
existentialism	renaissance art
fair trade	the small arms trade
feminism	sufism

Beginners
GUIDES

Opera
A Beginner's Guide

Alexandra Wilson

ONEWORLD
OXFORD

A Oneworld Paperback Original

Published by Oneworld Publications 2010

Copyright © Alexandra Wilson 2010

The moral right of Alexandra Wilson to be identified as the Author of this work
has been asserted by her in accordance with the Copyright, Designs and Patents
Act 1988

ISBN 978–1–85168–733–6

Typeset by Jayvee, Trivandrum, India
Cover design by Simon McFadden
Printed and bound by CPI Cox & Wyman, Reading RG1 8EX

Oneworld Publications
UK: 185 Banbury Road, Oxford, OX2 7AR, England
USA: 38 Greene Street, 4th Floor, New York, NY 10013, USA
www.oneworld-publications.com

Contents

Introduction   vii

1 A brief history of opera   1

2 Opera on and offstage   47

3 Opera and politics   79

4 Opera and identity: gender and
    race   107

Epilogue   130
Further reading   135
Bibliography   138
Recommended listening/viewing   144
Index   150

Introduction

What associations does the word 'opera' bring to mind for you? Grand opera houses built along classical lines, perhaps, their sumptuous interiors decked out in gold and red velvet? Audience members in black tie and ball gowns, quaffing champagne? Prohibitively expensive ticket prices? Or do you have a different conception of opera? Perhaps you imagine a free outside relay on an enormous screen in a packed piazza, a woman on a train listening to an I-Pod, a man listening to a live radio broadcast as he irons his shirts, a workshop in which school children devise an opera of their own, or an operatic classic in the soundtrack to a popular film or on a TV advertisement. Opera today brings to mind many and varied associations, although it is often still hampered by stereotypes that are in some cases outdated or unjustified.

Many people who have never been to see an opera seem to believe that it is something almost frightening, so often have they heard the words 'opera' and 'elitism' mentioned in the same breath. But what precisely about opera could be said to be elitist? Is the music itself too complex in some way for 'ordinary' people to understand? Do the plots of operas deal only with outdated upper-class preoccupations and are they somehow irrelevant to our lives today? Do you have to be fluent in foreign languages or highly educated in order to understand opera? Or is opera elitist because of the social trappings that surround it? On the other hand, might the whole concept of opera as elitist just be a lazy stereotype perpetuated by the media? In this book

I hope to show that opera can move and amuse us; that operas – even those written many centuries ago – can make us think about the most important issues of our times; and that opera is something that everyone can enjoy. In other words, my intention in this book is to try to demystify opera, challenging many of the popular misconceptions surrounding it and providing an introduction to the agendas that have governed the composition, production and reception of opera over the last four centuries. I hope that after reading this book, you will be in a better position to be critical about the operas you see at the theatre, on DVD or on film, and about how these have been interpreted.

There are several ways in which one could write a beginner's guide to opera. The most straightforward way of writing such a book would be simply to trace a narrative history of opera from its earliest beginnings to the present, providing plot summaries and composer biographies. But many books along these lines already exist and this guide seeks to do something a little more ambitious. My aim has been to strike a middle course between very general introductions to opera and specialized, academic texts, providing you – whether you're a music student or an opera enthusiast – with an introduction to the many lively, thought-provoking debates that have taken place about opera in recent decades. So, although the opening chapter of this guide provides a tour through the history and what we might call the mechanics of opera, the chapters that follow examine operas and operatic culture from a variety of critical perspectives, providing a sort of road-map of the diverse ways in which opera is studied and performed today. A further aim is to direct you towards the most significant literature on the topic in question so that you can extend your knowledge further.

The study of opera has changed a great deal in recent years. In the earlier twentieth century, opera was not, generally speaking, prioritized by scholars researching, teaching and writing about the history of music. Whereas non-texted musical works – and symphonies in particular – were regarded as serious music, most operas were not. Opera was regarded as less worthy of critical attention for a variety of reasons, not least because its sheer popularity with audiences meant that it straddled the boundary between art and entertainment in a way that seemed problematic. Many academics and critics also disparaged opera as a sort of impure or hybrid art-form that was neither pure music nor pure drama, and because its status as a collaborative art-form meant that it flew in the face of ideas developed during the nineteenth century about authorship and genius.

To express this concept in simple terms, a symphony by Beethoven, for instance, was composed by Beethoven alone and could be said to be an expression of his unique artistic vision. However, we couldn't really say the same of an opera by Beethoven's contemporary Rossini. On any individual opera, Rossini would have worked with a librettist (the person who wrote the words), a director, a choreographer, a set designer and various other interested parties. All of these people would have had a hand in shaping the opera that eventually reached the stage, as might the singers for whom Rossini originally envisaged the opera's roles. Opera could also be seen as more problematic than other types of music because operas have not necessarily been regarded as inviolable texts. To explain what I mean by this, it's helpful once again to draw a comparison between an opera and a symphony. Interpretative aspects of a Beethoven symphony might vary from performance to performance – there will always be small variations in terms of tempo, dynamics and so forth. However, the notes themselves will always be the same – it would be unheard of for an orchestra to start rewriting Beethoven's score. Operas, on the other hand, have historically been much more likely to be cut, adapted or embellished in performance; indeed, in Rossini's time, a certain degree of improvisation by the singers was considered the norm.

Today, scepticism about whether opera is a worthy subject
of study has largely disappeared, as the study of music has
broadened in recent decades to encompass a wider range of
musics, including pop and world music. Operas are far more
likely to feature prominently on a university music syllabus than
would have been the case twenty years ago; indeed, opera is
now at the heart of the study of music and a wide variety of
different critical approaches are applied to it. (It is telling that,
among the major musicological periodicals, there are several
specialist journals dedicated to opera, whereas there are none
specifically devoted to the symphony or the concerto.) This shift
can be attributed to a number of developments that have taken
place within the Humanities more broadly over the last few
decades. As well as analysing art-works as 'texts', scholars have
become increasingly interested in investigating the contexts that
shaped their objects of study, whether these be musical works,
novels, plays or paintings. Furthermore, there has been a
growing tendency in recent years towards scholarly approaches
that blur the boundaries between traditional disciplines. Opera,
as an art-form that combines text, music, visual spectacle and
movement, lends itself particularly well to these interdiscipli-
nary, contextual, cultural approaches. The study of opera is now
informed by approaches drawn from disciplines as varied as
sociology, gender studies, psychoanalysis and even medicine.

Whereas past generations, if they had studied operas at all,
would have been likely to have focused primarily upon how they
functioned musically and dramatically, scholars today are as likely
to be interested in the social, political or cultural contexts that
shaped a particular work, or how an opera has been received by
audiences, critics and performers. These new approaches have
allowed scholars to shed new light on familiar works, although
the range of operas being studied has also broadened to include a
greater number of works from outside the traditional Classical-
Romantic canon, including early operas and progressive

twentieth- and twenty-first-century operas. All of these developments have made the study of opera far more exciting.

The first chapter in this book provides a succinct overview
of operatic history, introducing you to key composers and works
and to how operas function musically and dramatically. (Here,
as elsewhere in the book, highlighted textboxes are used to
introduce key concepts and important terminology.) This paves
the way for subsequent chapters, which examine operas and
operatic culture from a variety of critical perspectives. In
keeping with the recent developments in opera studies
mentioned above, my main aim in the rest of the book is to help
you to understand the political, social and cultural agendas that
shaped operas, their production and their reception. Chapter
Two examines the processes by which an opera comes to the
stage and considers the politics of opera production. It introduces you to current debates about the relative merits of modern
and traditional stagings. Do operas from the past need to be
updated in order to speak to a contemporary audience?
Alternatively, should we aim to recreate the original performance conditions of opera, where the evidence survives? These
are topical and controversial questions that are of interest to
opera audiences as much as to opera directors and historians. I
also consider debates surrounding the practicalities and implications of transferring opera to film.

In Chapter Three I turn to political issues. Throughout
history, the operatic stage has been a forum for politics and
controversy, with composers and librettists either supporting or
critiquing the regime in power. Here I examine how composers
and librettists have treated political issues (sometimes using
operas as vehicles for propaganda) and how operas have, in turn,
been politicized through reception. A key case study is Verdi's
involvement in the drive for Italian unification, how he
conveyed political messages through his works and was adopted
as a political hero, and why his operas were censored. However,

I also introduce recent scholarly debates which suggest that the 'Verdi myth' was to some extent invented retrospectively, for political reasons, by the composer's biographers, illustrating that we need to be cautious about reading simple political messages into works from the past. Verdi's successor Puccini, meanwhile, presents an interesting paradox regarding the politicization of opera: he has often been presented as an apolitical composer and yet his operas were strongly politicized in his own day. Conversely a composer whose works have been politicized since his death – in ways that would have surpassed his wildest imaginings – is Richard Wagner. I conclude the chapter by discussing the extent to which the adoption of Wagner's works by the Nazis in the 1930s and 1940s should be viewed as having retrospectively tainted his works in some way.

The subject of Chapter Four is cultural politics: I examine the ways in which opera composers and librettists have portrayed women and people from cultures distant from their own. Operas throughout history have, for the most part, been composed by men. I explore how this has affected the way in which women have been portrayed in opera, asking whether composers had a conscious misogynist agenda, or whether they were simply following society's conventions or, indeed, operatic conventions. Another operatic topic often deemed politically contentious today is the treatment by many Western composers of Eastern subjects. Here I take as a case study Puccini's *Madama Butterfly*, examining whether the work should be viewed as imperialist or even racist, whether it is simply a product of its times, or whether Puccini even arguably expresses sympathy for the plight of his Japanese characters. You will be introduced to relevant feminist, post-feminist and post-colonial debates that can help us to understand this and other operas, but I also explore the idea that we should perhaps be cautious in interpreting art-works that are several centuries old through twenty-first-century eyes.

The inspiration to write this book came from teaching numerous students over the past fourteen years, at the universities of Oxford, Birmingham, and Newcastle upon Tyne, the Open University and Oxford Brookes University. In particular it has been shaped by the 'Opera and Politics' module that I have taught at Oxford Brookes since 2006 and by stimulating conversations I have had with individual students, especially those working on opera-related dissertations. I would like to thank the editors at Oneworld Publications for commissioning this title and giving me an opportunity to introduce the exciting world of opera to an even larger community of students and music lovers. On a personal note, I must offer thanks, as ever, to my husband, Andrew Timms, for his love and support.

Alexandra Wilson

1

A brief history of opera

As explained in the Introduction, this book is intended to be not so much a narrative history of opera as an introduction to the varied critical debates that surround the art-form today. However, in order to understand these debates, it is important to have some knowledge of the factors that shaped opera's birth, dissemination, development and (arguable) decline. The purpose of this chapter, then, is to introduce you to these events, while highlighted textboxes introduce you to key operatic concepts and important terminology. To tell the story of over four hundred years of operatic history in a matter of pages is a challenging prospect: indeed, whole books have been devoted to individual periods of operatic history. So it is inevitable that this chapter is something of a 'whistle-stop tour', focusing upon selected key moments in the history of the art-form. For a more detailed coverage of the history of opera in specific countries or centuries, or the oeuvre of individual composers, I suggest that you consult the further reading that I have recommended at the end of the book.

Operatic beginnings

Opera was born in Italy over four hundred years ago, and its roots can be traced specifically to late sixteenth-century Florence, a city buzzing with ideas and creativity at that time.

Over the previous century an astonishing outpouring of art, architecture, literature and scientific investigation had thrived in Florence under the patronage of wealthy rulers such as the Medici family, but there was a feeling that music had not kept up with the modernizing spirit of the times. So, in the 1570s a group of intellectuals, musicians and poets who have come to be known as 'The Florentine Camerata' began to meet regularly to discuss the state of music and how it might be reformed. Like many artists and thinkers of their day, the members of the Camerata believed that the way to move forwards was to look backwards and take inspiration from the Ancient World. They proposed Greek drama – which they believed to have been sung rather than spoken (although they had no firm evidence) – as a model for the future of Italian music.

Much of the music of the sixteenth century was polyphonic music, in which different vocal lines worked independently, overlapping with one another in ways that meant the text was often difficult to make out. The members of the Camerata believed that words ought to take precedence over music, and discussed new approaches to text setting in which the words might be expressed more clearly and dictate the rhythms of the music. They advocated the use of a style of music known as 'monody', in which a single vocal line was supported by a simple accompaniment, making the words easy to hear. Over the next fifteen years, the Camerata debated ways of combining this new approach to vocal music with drama in order to create a form of entertainment that they believed would replicate what the ancient Greeks experienced. However, the early operas were also influenced by more recent forms of theatre, such as the sixteenth-century court *intermedi* – musical entertainments that were performed between the acts of a play, providing light relief from the main dramatic fare on offer.

The Camerata's ideas were developed further in the 1590s by the most important Florentine patron of music of the day,

Jacopo Corsi. He encouraged the composer Jacopo Peri and the poet Ottavio Rinuccini to put the Camerata's ideas into practice, and in around 1597 the pair collaborated to produce the first complete staged work in the new style, a work called *Dafne*, based on the Greek legend of Apollo and his unrequited love for the nymph Daphne. At the turn of a new century, opera was born.

AN INTRODUCTION TO RECITATIVE AND ARIA

Relatively early in the history of opera, the basic 'building blocks' of opera – recitative and arias – were established. Recitative is a cross between singing and speaking. It allows a lot of text to be transmitted rapidly and is used when composer and librettist need to impart a lot of information and move the plot along. By the eighteenth century, two different types of recitative had developed – accompanied recitative (with light orchestral accompaniment) and *secco* (literally 'dry') recitative, accompanied only by occasional chords, usually played on a harpsichord and perhaps a few bass stringed instruments. (This type would later die out in the nineteenth century.)

Put simply, whereas recitative conveys action, arias are more reflective: the action halts as a singer reflects upon what has just happened, upon a piece of information he or she has received, or upon his or her own personal state of mind. Arias are essentially the 'tuneful' parts of an opera. An aria is sung by a soloist but there are of course also scenes in which several characters sing together. Duets, trios, quartets and larger ensembles work in the same way, dramatically speaking, as arias – they allow for a moment of repose and reflection.

Unfortunately, the music for *Dafne* has been lost, but the first opera to have survived is another work by Peri and Rinuccini called *Euridice*, written in 1600 to celebrate the marriage of the Florentine noblewoman Maria de Medici to King Henri IV of

France. The Medicis used the opportunity as a way of impressing not only their French visitors but their political rivals from neighbouring Italian states. (Italy was at this time not a united country but a collection of small dukedoms and princedoms.) The new form of entertainment must have delighted and captivated all those who attended. Other noblemen, equally keen to show off, began to commission operas to celebrate weddings, coronations, funerals, births, birthdays and military victories, and generally to demonstrate the wealth of their courts. One such nobleman was Duke Vincenzo Gonzaga of Mantua, who had been impressed by the lavish spectacle he had witnessed in Florence. The composer he employed in his court was one destined to live on far more successfully in the history books than Peri – Claudio Monteverdi.

Monteverdi's first opera for the Mantua court, *Orfeo* (1607), written with the poet Alessandro Striggio, was based on the same source as Peri's *Euridice* – the legend of Orpheus, the musician with such powers that he could bring his lover Euridice back from the dead. Not only was this an appropriate subject for musical treatment, but the subject matter of such works allowed composers to flatter their patrons by likening them to the gods and goddesses of ancient Greek myth. *Orfeo* was a more ambitious work than Peri's *Euridice* and its score more harmonically complex and melodically engaging. Alongside mixing solo and ensemble numbers, choruses and dances, Monteverdi exploited the rich instrumental resources available to him at the Mantua court, using trombones, bass viols and cornetts to bring the underworld to life. (Monteverdi was unusually precise for his time in specifying which instruments he wanted to be used.) All of these features, when combined with extravagant costumes, sets and stage machinery, created a work that was unprecedented in musical and dramatic expressiveness, guaranteed to impress Duke Gonzaga's political rivals.

So, the earliest operas were performed in front of small elite groups of spectators (and created by composers and poets who were effectively court servants), but opera was soon to reach out to a larger audience. Monteverdi's career clearly illustrates this shift from private to public opera. When Duke Vincenzo died, Monteverdi left the Gonzaga court and moved to Venice, where he took up the post of 'Maestro di Capella' at St Mark's Cathedral in 1613. Although much of his time was occupied with writing sacred works, as time went on he acquired the freedom to branch out into writing secular music, including opera. But opera in Venice was different. Venice was a Republic, and without a single ruling family there was no place for court opera along the lines Monteverdi had experienced in Mantua. However, the city was an important commercial centre, which welcomed many foreign merchants, businessmen, dignitaries and aristocrats on the 'Grand Tour', and the demand for entertainment was high, particularly during the carnival, which took place each February. After a touring company brought an opera to Venice for the first time during the carnival season of 1637 (Benedetto Ferrari and Francesco Manelli's *Andromeda*), some enterprising Venetian impresarios came up with the idea of setting up opera houses and charging the public for the hire of boxes on a subscription system. However, it would be an over-exaggeration to depict seventeenth-century Venetian opera as opera 'for the masses' – the opera houses were owned by noble families, opera-goers were still from privileged backgrounds and ticket prices were high.

Operas ceased to be one-off events and became regular occurrences, often playing for an entire season, and with opera now a commercial enterprise, box office appeal became crucial. Although the earliest Venetian operas continued to be based on classical mythology, composers increasingly turned towards historical subjects with more recognizably human characters. (The priority for a composer was no longer to appeal to the vanity of a ruler; indeed, the new type of opera sometimes even depicted rulers as corrupt and greedy.) They also had to be more economical than the early court operas – commercially run theatres could not afford the sort of lavish sets that were used in the courts. Large-scale permanent orchestras were also too expensive for most theatres, meaning that composers had to scale back the orchestration that they called for. However, a benefit of using a smaller instrumental group was that the voices were shown off to greater effect, and as the seventeenth century progressed composers began to include more and more arias in their opera scores.

Monteverdi embraced these new trends in his opera *L'incoronazione di Poppea* ('The Coronation of Poppea', 1642–3), which told the story of the love affair between the Roman emperor Nero and his mistress Poppea. This work was very different to Monteverdi's earlier court opera *Orfeo*. It was a story full of lust and violence: obeying Poppea's commands, Nero divorces his wife, exiles Poppea's husband and condemns the philosopher Seneca to death. The opera's score represents another change in the new operatic style, towards greater lyricism, straightforward harmonies, strong rhythms and vivid musical characterization. These characteristics are summed up particularly well in the sensuous closing love duet between Nero and his triumphant mistress, although historians have suggested that this duet was added after the first performance and was probably not actually written by Monteverdi. Although this might sound surprising, it was relatively common for operas of this period to be written by teams of composers; such a composite work was known as a *pasticcio*.

A 'star system' for singers soon emerged in Venice that prefigured modern notions of celebrity – one of the most successful and celebrated singers of the era was the soprano Anna Renzi. The success of an opera depended increasingly upon the virtuoso qualities of the lead performers: parts were written to show off the strengths of an individual's voice, and the most successful singers acquired the power to dictate not only their role but how long their scenes should be and even which other singers should appear in the production. The most successful singers were typically paid more than the composers whose works they performed, often several times more, and their names appeared more prominently on publicity materials than those of composers or librettists. Opera during the seventeenth century was a genuinely collaborative art, a partnership between composer, poet, scenographer, performers, theatre owner and impresario. However, the partnership was by no means an equal one – there was a clear hierarchy, with singers at the top. As we shall see, the dynamics of this relationship between different creative agents was to change at various times during opera's history.

Exporting opera abroad

The seasons for commercial opera in Italy were short and in the intervening periods, opera companies would go on tour. It would not be long before opera would extend its influence beyond the Italian peninsula. By the mid seventeenth century opera was not only spreading throughout the Italian states but was also beginning to be exported to northern Europe: in particular, Italian composers began to establish themselves in German courts. However, Italian opera was not welcomed everywhere. When works by Cavalli, Sacrati and Rossi were taken to Paris in the 1640s, they were greeted with hostility. France had its own indigenous forms of theatrical entertainment and many aspects of Italian opera ran counter to French tastes. French composers, led by Jean-Baptiste Lully (who had actually been born in Italy but who spent his adult life in France), developed their own musico-dramatic genres such as the *Tragédie en musique*, leading to heated debates in contemporary pamphlets about the merits of the two national styles.

French opera developed its own particular characteristics and structure: a French opera was usually in five acts (preceded by an overture and allegorical prologue) and broken up by a number of *divertissements* – dances, choral songs or instrumental 'symphonies' – which were performed between the acts. The idea of glorifying a ruler, which the Italians were to some extent abandoning, remained an important feature of French operatic culture. Lully based his *Tragédies en musique* on classical mythology or medieval romance, with the hero often serving as an allegory for his employer Louis XIV, the Sun King. Indeed, the King took a very active involvement in shaping the operas that were performed at his court, intervening in the choice of subjects Lully set. Furthermore, Louis's enjoyment of dancing led to the distinctive French tradition of including lavish ballets, in which he himself would perform. The voices used in French opera were different too – French composers shunned the castrato so beloved of Italian opera composers and audiences (a topic to which I shall return presently), preferring to use a distinctive high tenor voice known as an *haute contre*.

Another country to develop its own distinctive forms of musico-dramatic entertainment was England. The English 'semi opera' developed by Henry Purcell and his contemporaries in the second half of the seventeenth century drew upon influences such as the masque (a genre of courtly entertainment that blended dance, spectacle and an element of narrative) as well as a variety of French and Italian musical styles. Purcell's best known work in this style is *Dido and Aeneas*, set to a libretto by Nahum Tate and based upon an episode recounted in Virgil's *Aeneid*, in which Prince Aeneas is tricked by a sorceress into abandoning his lover, Queen Dido of Carthage. The opera is full of lively and picturesque choruses of witches and sailors (many in a simple homophonic, or chordal, style), but it also features expressive arias, most notably Dido's famous 'lament', set over a ground bass (a bass-line that is repeated time after

THE OPERA OVERTURE

An overture is a piece of orchestral music that the audience hears before the curtain rises. Its purpose is to whet the audience's appetite for what will follow, or – more prosaically – to act as a call to attention, giving the audience time to settle down before the action starts. Initially, overtures were independent instrumental works, distinct from the operas that they preceded – this was true of works by Purcell and Handel, for example. They were often structured in contrasting sections (often drawn from traditional dance forms), rather like an instrumental suite. Later on, overtures became more intimately connected to their respective operas, either setting an appropriate mood (or range of contrasting moods) or including melodies that the audience would hear later on. This approach was taken to extremes in the operetta genre, notably in the works of Gilbert and Sullivan, in which the overtures are potpourris of all the main themes the audience will hear later on. By the early twentieth century, the overture was starting to become less important. Most of Puccini's works, for example, throw us straight into the action: the curtain rises immediately, the characters can be seen bustling around the stage, and within just a few bars of music they will start to sing.

time). Home-grown opera did not develop to any great extent in England, however, and it would not be until the twentieth century that English opera really took off. That said, foreign operas were performed in Britain with great success, as we shall see in the next section.

Serious opera in the eighteenth century

Despite the gradual development of different national schools of opera, Italian opera continued to extend its influence. By the eighteenth century, Italian opera had become the predominant form of aristocratic entertainment all over Europe, gaining a foothold in countries as far flung as England and Russia. The genre of opera that dominated the courts and large civic theatres of the day was *opera seria* – a form of serious opera the conventions of which were developed around the year 1700 and that enjoyed its heyday between the 1720s and the 1780s. *Opera seria* developed in response to widespread calls for the literary reform of earlier Italian opera, which was widely believed to be becoming corrupt, with its excessively complicated plots, supernatural characters and emphasis upon visual spectacle. The poet Apostolo Zeno developed a new type of libretto, based upon historical subjects, with condensed casts and logically unfolding plots. Yet more reforms were carried out by Pietro Metastasio, a librettist who worked closely with composers in producing texts that lent themselves well to musical setting in such a way as to make the most of dramatic climaxes. He codified a number of archetypal narrative scenarios and his libretti were set hundreds of times during the eighteenth century, both by Italian composers and by foreign composers writing in the Italian style. It's interesting to note that in the eighteenth century, libretti were endlessly recycled by different composers, whereas in later periods a libretto would be written for a specific composer and used just once.

Many of the most famous Italian *opera seria* composers of the eighteenth century have names that have long been lost to the mists of the time – opportunities are rare these days to see an opera by Leo, Vinci, Jommelli or Traetta, for instance. Interestingly, the operas in this style that have survived tend to be those that were composed by non-Italian composers. The fact that Italian opera was becoming a truly international art by the eighteenth century is something that is illustrated particularly well by what may strike you as the rather curious career of George Frideric Handel, a German composer who travelled to

LIBRETTO

The text for an opera is called a libretto (Italian for 'little book'). Although a few composers, such as Wagner, have written their own libretti, most have worked in conjunction with one or more professional librettists. In recent centuries it has been common practice for the librettist to supply the words before the composer starts to write the music, although this was not always the case for early operas, which were often put together at great speed. Some operas are original stories, but most are based on pre-existing literary sources, such as plays or novels. You might wonder why a composer couldn't just set a play as written. One reason is that it takes much longer to sing words than it does to say them, so the amount of text in a libretto will be considerably less than in a play of the same duration. The librettist usually puts the text into verse form, with a rhyme scheme and lines of a regular length, so that it fits conventional musical phrasing. Furthermore, in an opera libretto, words and sentences tend to be repeated for emphasis in a way that makes sense when set to music but that would seem nonsensical in a play. However, some composers from the late nineteenth century onwards have experimented with setting short plays as they stand, or even passages of prose.

Italy during his youth and who subsequently spent much of his career in London. While living there, he wrote operas in the Italian style (with a few 'French' elements) and with Italian dialogue for the entertainment of an English-speaking audience. Handel's first opera for London was *Rinaldo*, premiered in 1711, and he would write another forty operas for the city over the following three decades, many based upon episodes from Greek and Roman history.

By this time, operas were lengthy affairs, often lasting three hours, but audience members were not expected to give their rapt attention to the entire performance. Instead, they would eat, drink, talk, gamble, conduct business and carry on liaisons, turning their attention to the matters on stage only at the most dramatically and musically interesting moments. Audiences also did not hold back from expressing their opinions of particular singers. Florid vocal decoration was the fashion and the vehicle for this was an aria form known as *da capo*, which, put simply, might be represented thus: A B A'. The character would sing an initial section of text (section A), which would be followed by a second section (section B) which contrasted with it in terms of both dramatic and musical mood. The A section was then repeated, but this time with improvised decorations, with the aim of showing off the voice to maximum effect and soliciting applause through runs, ornaments and spectacular vocal leaps. Singers were judged on how well they could improvise and a singer who simply repeated the A section as written in the score would be likely to be booed off the stage or might even be pelted with rotten tomatoes. Audience members would attend the same opera night after night and would expect singers to embellish their arias differently on each occasion.

It was considered the norm in this period for singers to take considerable liberties with the composer's score – for example by inserting arias from completely different operas (these were known as 'suitcase arias' because a singer carried them around from opera to opera). This idea seems quite strange to us today – we might expect a composer to feel insulted if the singers didn't perform his or her music as written! However, most composers of this period condoned and facilitated performer freedom, realizing that allowing a star singer to put his or her own imprint on an opera would be key to its commercial success. We should also remember that this was an age in which composers didn't have as strong a sense of 'ownership' of their music as their later counterparts. Whereas many nineteenth- and twentieth-century composers perceived their compositions as finished, definitive works and expected performers to adhere to their carefully notated performance directions, this would have been, by and large, an alien idea to earlier composers.

In the eighteenth century composers took a more free and easy attitude towards their music. They did not treat their own compositions as inviolable texts and each work was not expected to be a distinctive work of art, as would become the case in the later nineteenth century. (Indeed, composers of the early eighteenth century often had to write so much music for their patrons that recycling sections of earlier works – albeit retailored to a new context – became a practical necessity.) The greater degree of flexibility inherent in the performance of opera during the eighteenth century means that modern singers are placed in something of a conundrum when they perform this repertory today. Should they also embellish *da capo* arias differently each time they perform them, or perhaps even insert 'suitcase arias' into the operas they perform? Few classical singers today are used to improvising on a daily basis in the way that came as second nature to singers of the eighteenth century. However, to perform operas of this period following the notes in the score to the letter would certainly not be in the correct spirit of this repertory.

Singers still had more prestige during this period than composers and received better pay. The *prima donna* (leading lady) and *primo uomo* (leading man) were the celebrities of their day, and continued to be given higher status and billing on promotional posters than the composer himself. The most celebrated singers of all were the castrati – the most famous being two singers known as Farinelli (the pseudonym for Carlo Maria Broschi) and Senesino (Francesco Bernardi), who could command enormous fees. The castrati were promising boy singers who were castrated before their voices broke, a procedure that left them with distinctive voices which were high and agile yet very powerful. Curiously to us perhaps, this strangely emasculated vocal type was considered heroic in the early eighteenth century (and female audience members reportedly found castrati highly desirable); thus, the most important male roles in Italian operas of this period were always sung by castrati. The castrati also sometimes took on female roles, for instance in cities such as Rome where women were forbidden to appear on the operatic stage.

The operatic taste for the castrato was to decline by the late eighteenth century and in the nineteenth century the heroic roles would be taken, instead, by high tenor voices. However, the castration practice lingered on in certain contexts. The Sistine Chapel, for instance, continued to use castrati throughout the nineteenth century, until the Pope outlawed the practice in 1903: it is even possible to hear recordings of one of the last Sistine castrati, Alessandro Moreschi, made in the early 1900s. Today the operatic roles originally written for castrati must either be transposed to a lower key or be performed by women or counter-tenors (male singers with a high vocal range, achieved through the use of falsetto). However, any of these solutions to the problem is a compromise: no voice type available today resembles the distinctive timbre of the castrato voice. An interesting digital attempt to recreate the sound of the castrato voice was made in the 1994 film *Farinelli* (directed by Gérard Corbiau), in which the voices of a female soprano and a counter-tenor were electronically blended together.

Opera seria survived to the end of the eighteenth century across Europe, proving particularly popular in German-speaking countries. However, the genre was increasingly criticized for its emphasis upon vocal virtuosity (often at the expense of dramatic credibility), as well as for the use of the unnatural castrato voice. Christoph Willibald Gluck (1714–87) led a movement for opera to become more natural and for the music to serve the dramatic action rather than the other way around. In the preface to his opera *Alceste* (first performed in 1767) he complained about the 'abuses' that he wished to strip from opera: *da capo* arias, displays of vocal virtuosity for its own sake and the tyranny of singers. In

VOICE TYPES IN OPERA

For many types of music, such as choral music, voices are grouped into four categories: soprano (high female), alto (low female), tenor (high male) and bass (low male). (Occasionally gender divisions are blurred – you might sometimes hear a male alto or a female tenor.) You may also come across 'intermediate' voice parts: a mezzo-soprano straddles the soprano and alto ranges, and a baritone is mid way between a tenor and a bass. In opera, yet more subtleties are drawn, denoting the specific range, tone colour and timbre required. For instance, a particular soprano role may be referred to as a *'coloratura'* role, meaning that the singer has to perform florid music that calls for great agility in the upper range.

Over opera's history, conventions have developed that associate voice types with particular sorts of character. The heroic roles that dominate the action tend to be given to singers with higher voices. So, the young lovers in an opera will generally be sung by a soprano and a tenor, with the lower voices being used for older characters or for authority figures (parents, kings and so on). 'Down to earth' characters are typically sung by mezzos or baritones, who have the most 'natural' voices.

place of these characteristics, Gluck favoured simple melodies and accompaniment, and a clear expression of the text, which had really been the point of opera from the start. The mid-century reforms were taken up by later eighteenth-century *opera seria* composers such as Mozart, whose serious operas include *Idomeneo* (1781) and *La clemenza di Tito* (1791).

The rise of comic opera

In parallel with *opera seria*, a new form of comic opera, known as *opera buffa*, had emerged in Italy (specifically in Naples) in the first decades of the eighteenth century. Comic operas started as comic interludes that were performed between the acts of serious works (known as *intermezzi* – the best known of which was Pergolesi's *La serva padrona*, first performed in 1733), but ultimately developed into a full evening's entertainment in their own right. *Opere serie* were usually based upon mythological subject matter or the lives of kings and queens, were serious and heroic in tone, and included a great deal of florid, virtuosic singing. *Opere buffe*, on the other hand, were more light-hearted, primarily involved ordinary characters rather than gods and rulers, and often took a satirical approach to social hierarchies. But despite *opera buffa*'s relatively free attitude towards social mores, it was a genre that was strictly codified in terms of dramatic and musical conventions. Standardized plot devices, musical styles and stock characters – many derived from the traditional Italian genre of theatre known as the *commedia dell'arte* – were transported from opera to opera, rather as they are in modern day pantomime. And just as in pantomime, audiences expected certain conventions and found them reassuring: particular musical conventions signalled to the audience what to expect from a character. An *opera buffa* would generally contain a mixture of comic characters (such as a buffoon-type male character who sang in a 'patter' style – almost like very fast speaking) and more serious characters, whose music was more complex to sing, often metaphorically denoting their higher social status. On the whole, however, *opera buffa* placed less emphasis upon vocal display for its own sake and more upon human situations, and strong acting skills were demanded from the performers.

Many composers of *opera buffa* who were very successful in their day have, like those of *opera seria*, now been forgotten – unfortunately we rarely have a chance nowadays to watch or hear the operas of Hasse, Paisiello or Salieri, for example. However, three comic operas written by Mozart, in collaboration with the librettist Lorenzo Da Ponte, remain central to the modern operatic repertoire: *Le nozze di Figaro* (*The Marriage of Figaro*) (1786), *Don Giovanni* (1787) and *Così fan tutte* ('Thus do They All', 1790). All three operas are striking both for their beautiful music and for their nuanced musical characterization. *Le nozze di Figaro* is a good example of an opera with a political element, telling the story of a group of clever servants who outwit their master. This was regarded as a scandalous topic – bear in mind that it was written in the troubled times leading up to the French Revolution – to the extent that the play upon which the opera was based (by the French playwright Pierre-Augustin Beaumarchais) had been banned. I shall return to this opera in Chapter Three.

Don Giovanni shows that 'comic' operas were not always entirely comic. It tells the story of the legendary lothario Don Juan – Don Giovanni is the Italian version of his name – who eventually falls victim to divine retribution. The original literary source for this work is thought to have been a seventeenth-century play by a monk called Tirso de Molina, but his story had subsequently been retold many times, in plays by such notable figures as Molière and Goldoni, as well as in prose, poetry, music and even dance. In Mozart and Da Ponte's version of the legend, Don Giovanni is a serial seducer. At the beginning of the opera he attempts to rape a young noblewoman called Donna Anna; her father, the Commendatore, defends her honour and is killed by her would-be attacker in a duel. Don Giovanni then continues with his philandering ways, attempting to woo a young peasant girl called Zerlina as she is about to marry her fiancé, Masetto. In the second act we are introduced to Donna Elvira, a woman seduced and abandoned by the Don in the past, who is determined to expose his misdemeanours. Finally, Don Giovanni, sheltering in a cemetery at night-time, spots the statue of the Commendatore that adorns the old man's tombstone and contemptuously invites it to dinner. The statue later turns up at the Don's house, chastising him for his sins; Don Giovanni is carried off by devils to hell.

This opera, which has a range of comic and more serious characters, illustrates the conventions of *opera buffa* very clearly, and also how music could be used to represent different strata of social prestige. Don Giovanni's servant Leporello is the typical comic bass who sings in a patter style. Zerlina and her fiancé are humble countryfolk, so their music is less virtuosic than that of the noblewoman Donna Anna. This opera also offers a very clear illustration of another important structural convention of *opera buffa*. Mozart and Da Ponte use musical and dramatic structures in such a way as to build and then diffuse dramatic tension at particular points across the course of the opera. One of the most important moments in an opera of this period is the mid-point finale. In the case of *Don Giovanni* (a two-act opera) this falls at the end of the first act; in a four-act opera it would fall at the end of act two but fulfil the same function – to wind up the dramatic tension just before the interval, leaving the audience in suspense and whetting their appetites to see how the conundrums the characters find themselves in will be resolved. The mid-point finale in a Mozart opera is a fast-paced, extended scene in which most or all of the characters are involved and are able to confront one another. It is the dramatic high point of the opera, the moment of maximum confusion (possibly involving disguise or some sort of mistaken identity), and typically includes a shock revelation, further intensifying the dramatic tension. All of these characteristics are very easily identified in the mid-point finale of *Don Giovanni*, which takes place at a ball at the Don's house. Immediately a conflict is set up as Donna Anna, Donna Elvira and Don Ottavio (Donna Anna's fiancé) arrive disguised behind masks in order to seek revenge on the Don. The action reaches a crescendo when Zerlina is heard to scream offstage. She rushes onto the stage in distress following an attempted seduction by the Don, who tries to blame his servant Leporello. The finale ends with Donna Anna, Donna Elvira and Don Ottavio taking off their masks and warning Don Giovanni that his misdemeanours have been discovered and that vengeance is nigh.

Mozart uses musical devices in a variety of ways to help build the dramatic tension. Unity between characters is demonstrated by their singing the same words in unison (such as when the three interlopers hear Zerlina screaming and resolve to come to her aid). However, at other points in the finale Mozart demonstrates moments of dramatic dissent by having characters sing different words at the same time. By the end of the scene, all characters are singing, but a variety of different emotions are being expressed, either in turn or simultaneously. Zerlina, her suitor Masetto and the interlopers are united in denouncing Don Giovanni and calling for vengeance, while he and Leporello, meanwhile, express their confusion and fear. The fact that the individual words are, at some moments, difficult for a listener to make out is a deliberate strategy to create a sense of maximum confusion. By the end of the finale, nothing has really been resolved. It will not be until the very end of the opera, in the much shorter finale proper, that the dramatic tension is finally diffused. In this instance, Don Giovanni has been dragged down to hell in the penultimate scene. In the very last scene, all the characters who have been wronged by the Don join together in an ensemble in which they comment on his fate: each explains how their life can now return to normal. The opera ends on a moralistic note, with the characters joining together to tell the audience that this is what happens to those who commit evil acts.

As well as writing in the Italian style, Mozart branched out on several occasions into writing a distinctively German type of opera, the most famous example being his work *The Magic Flute* (*Die Zauberflöte*), written in 1791, the last year of his life. *The Magic Flute* was not technically an opera but a *Singspiel*, a new form of German comic opera that had developed in the 1760s. Emperor Joseph II of Austria promoted the development of

German opera, establishing in 1778 a company specifically devoted to it, the 'National Singspiel'. *Singspiel* differed from Italian opera in several important ways. Firstly, a *Singspiel* would be sung in German – the language of the people for whom it was being performed. Secondly, whereas the arias in Italian operas were linked together by recitative, a *Singspiel* interspersed arias with spoken dialogue, rather like a modern musical. These features made the genre more accessible for a wide social audience than Italian opera. Whereas Italian operas were attended by the aristocracy in Vienna, the *Singspiel* was a form of entertainment performed primarily to a less privileged audience. Many *Singspiel* were performed at the Theater auf der Wieden, a relatively unfashionable theatre, which presented a range of different sorts of entertainment.

It was appropriate that Mozart should have used this new, more democratic genre of German opera for *The Magic Flute*, for its very subject matter is concerned with democratic ideals. The opera is rather like a fairy tale and recounts the story of a journey, an individual's quest for knowledge. It has often been read as an allegory for contemporary Enlightenment ideals, which placed emphasis upon reason and human knowledge. The libretto (by Emanuel Schikaneder) is full of symbolism about darkness and light, as the characters move, throughout the course of the opera, from an unenlightened to an enlightened state. This interest in using opera as a vehicle for politics (which I will discuss further in Chapter Three) was something that would continue into the nineteenth century, as would the development of distinctive national styles of opera.

Early nineteenth-century opera

During the nineteenth century, Italian operas – both serious and comic – continued to be composed in huge numbers. However, other national traditions began to develop which took the operatic art-form in starkly different directions. Like the symphony, operas reached extremes of size during this period and many of the works that are centrepieces of the operatic repertory today were composed during the nineteenth century. By the nineteenth century, every small Italian town had its opera house, although the most important theatres were to be found in larger cities such as Milan, Turin, Rome and Venice. Unlike France, where operatic life focused very much upon Paris, Italy had a decentralized operatic system because it was not a unified nation until the 1860s.

A new style of Italian opera was developed in the early nineteenth century by a group of composers led by Gioachino Rossini. He established a new set of structural conventions that would act as a sort of blueprint for other Italian composers writing during the early part of the nineteenth century. As we have already seen, composers throughout history developed new approaches to operatic language and expression that suited their evolving dramatic needs. In the early nineteenth century composers gradually began to abandon the three-part *da capo* aria that was so important during the eighteenth century, favouring a two-part aria form that allowed for a dramatic change of mood between the two sections.

Rossini's approach to constructing an operatic scene dominated by a single character was as follows. An introductory section would be followed by a slow, expressive aria (known as the *cantabile*), which allowed a character to reflect upon his or her situation. A transitional passage would bring about a change in mood, leading to a faster, more brilliant aria known as the *cabaletta*. This pattern allowed the action to move along more rapidly than the three-part *da capo* aria of the eighteenth century, since the composer was not obliged to return to the mood of the initial section of text. There was, however, still scope for the singer to embellish his or her music during the *cabaletta*, in order to show off the particular strengths of his or her voice. Scenes with two or more characters could be structured in a similar way. Rossini dominated the opera world from the 1810s to the 1830s, writing both comic and serious works. He wrote operas not only for Italy but also for France, and his works were exported all over Europe. Rossini's younger colleagues, Bellini and Donizetti, continued his innovations. The style of singing favoured during this period tends to be known as '*bel canto*', and emphasizes lyrical lines, legato (smoothly connected) phrasing and a seemingly effortless vocal technique even in highly ornamented passages. The orchestral accompaniment for such music tends to be discreet: all emphasis is upon the voice.

Composers during this period began to turn to ever more diverse kinds of literary subject. Operas based on classical legend were now rare in Italy (we have seen that the composers of *opera seria* were already rejecting such subjects in favour of historical topics). Bellini's *Norma* was set in Gaul during the Roman occupation, but early nineteenth-century operas more typically drew upon episodes from relatively more recent history – the Tudor period, for instance, in the case of Donizetti's *Anna Bolena* and *Maria Stuarda*. Composers also turned increasingly to the literature of their own day (although this was not unknown in the eighteenth century, as Mozart's use of the Figaro story by his contemporary Beaumarchais illustrates). A prime example is Donizetti's opera *Lucia di Lammermoor* (1835), based upon Sir Walter Scott's novel *The Bride of Lammermoor*, written just sixteen years earlier. The Scottish landscape of Scott's novel would have seemed highly exotic and appealing to Italian audiences at the time. Mists, mountains and dramatic landscapes were central to the Romantic aesthetic across Europe: a good example from the visual arts of this preoccupation can be seen in the paintings of the German artist Caspar David Friedrich (1774–1840).

German composers of the early nineteenth century, inspired by the preoccupations of contemporary novels and paintings, became particularly interested in supernatural subjects in which the spirit world and the mortal world confronted one another. E. T. A. Hoffmann's *Undine* (1816), for instance, deals with the typically Romantic theme of a love affair between a water spirit and a mortal. One of the most significant – and popular – early nineteenth-century German operas, meanwhile, was Weber's *Der Freischütz* (1821), usually translated as *The Marksman*, which was seized upon as a symbol of German national identity. The opera, set in Bohemia, tells the story of a shooting competition, arranged by a forester to decide who will marry his daughter, Agathe. Max, the hero, who loves Agathe, desperately accepts an offer of help from another character, Caspar, who has sold his soul to the Devil. Caspar obtains seven magic bullets for Max: six will reach their target but the seventh is controlled by the Devil. This opera included elements of the old *Singspiel* tradition (including spoken dialogue and folk-like choruses), but was distinctively Romantic in ambience, with its dark, forest setting, supernatural subject matter and atmospheric orchestration: the scene in the haunted Wolf's Glen particularly appealed to the Romantic imagination. Weber, along with contemporaries such as Spohr, began to use recurring musical motifs in a way that would pre-empt Wagner's later, more complex use of them.

As in earlier periods, French opera continued to be distinct from the Italian model, although there was a certain degree of cultural exchange between the two traditions in the early nineteenth century. We have already seen that Rossini spent time in Paris, and developed new approaches to composition during his time there. Verdi would also be influenced by the French operatic aesthetic from the middle of his career onwards. In turn, French composers incorporated some elements of the Italian vocal style into their compositions. However, what came to be known as French Grand Opera had a variety of characteristics that were distinct from operatic models elsewhere. 'Grand Operas' were customarily in four or five acts and contained a lavish ballet sequence (usually placed at the beginning of the second act), continuing a French preoccupation with dance on the operatic stage that, as we have seen, dated back to the days of Louis XIV. Grand Operas also typically called for large orchestras and impressive instrumental effects.

Grand Opera librettos were generally drawn from historical subjects and often dealt with the plight of notable individuals from the past. French opera had become highly political by the late eighteenth century (after the Revolution of 1789 many operas dealt with revolutionary subjects and some were highly propagandistic), and we can see the continuation of this preoccupation with challenging authority in the Grand Operas of the early nineteenth century. For instance, Daniel Auber's *La Muette de Portici* (1828), often regarded as the first true Grand Opera, is about a failed revolt in 1647 by the people of Naples against the occupying Spaniards. This opera ends with a character throwing herself into the lava of the erupting Mount Vesuvius. A scene like this would have demanded extravagant scenery and stage effects that reflected the early nineteenth-century French desire for visual spectacle. French Grand Operas also tended to boast crowd scenes that called for hundreds of performers. This preoccupation with opera on a literally grand scale continued until the mid nineteenth century, with elements of the style living on in later works by composers of French and other nationalities.

Two nineteenth-century greats

A particularly auspicious year in the history of opera was 1813. It saw the birth of Verdi and Wagner, two composers who could reasonably be said to have dominated nineteenth-century opera,

THE OPERA CHORUS

Opera choruses are large groups of singers who are not given individual character names but operate en masse. Choruses hark back to ancient Greek theatre: their purpose is to comment upon the things that are happening to the central characters. Opera choruses have been employed to varying degrees in different historical periods and in different national styles of opera. For instance, we might say that the eighteenth century was essentially an age of star soloists and that choruses came into their own in the nineteenth century, growing in size and being given increasingly sophisticated music and a more important role in the drama. Some of the Grand Operas of the nineteenth century by composers such as Auber, Meyerbeer and later Verdi (in the case of selected works, notably *Aida* (1871)) called for massive crowd scenes, ceremonies and processions. The singers who made up nineteenth-century opera choruses were usually recruited on an ad hoc basis and were not always particularly well trained or even necessarily able to read music. Composers were often frustrated by their technical limitations: Verdi made appeals for choruses to be properly trained and disciplined, to equip them for the sophisticated musical demands of his choral writing. Only from the twentieth century onwards did it become customary for opera companies to employ professional, full-time choruses.

but each of whom took the art-form in very different directions. Both men were composers whose works have become deeply embroiled in political debates and I shall return to these later in Chapter Three; here, however, I'll sketch a brief overview of their main operatic achievements. Many Italians today would probably still point to Giuseppe Verdi as the greatest of all Italian opera composers. He lived for most of his life in the region around Parma, in central Italy, although his operas were premiered in cities all over the Italian peninsula or even, in a few cases, abroad. Like many Italian composers of the nineteenth century, Verdi concentrated primarily on operatic composition. He also wrote some highly notable choral music, such as the *Requiem*, although this was criticized during his lifetime for simply being 'an opera in ecclesiastical garb'. His career was a long one: his first opera (*Oberto: conte di San Bonifacio*) was premiered in 1839 and his last (*Falstaff*) in 1893. Over the course of these five-and-a-half decades, Verdi wrote a huge number of operas, sometimes several per year (some of his earlier works are rarely performed today, but many of the works from his mid to late career continue to form the backbone of the contemporary operatic repertory). However, his rate of production slowed as his career progressed. This was not the result of laziness or a case of a composer resting upon his laurels; rather, Italian composers' attitude to operatic production was changing. In the early part of the century, composers such as Rossini had produced operas at a prolific rate, often because they were working to commission, but some of these operas could reasonably be said to be fairly similar to one another. Verdi, on the other hand, became increasingly interested in ensuring that each of his operas was distinct from the last, with its own atmosphere and its own musical sound world, or *tinta*.

Verdi's works became ever more sophisticated as he began to incorporate a range of foreign musical influences and, crucially, as he strove tirelessly for a greater degree of dramatic realism. He became frustrated with the two-part aria form that the Italian composers of the earlier nineteenth century had developed, with its slow first section and its fast, brilliant *cabaletta*, because he believed it to be dramatically limiting and because it seemed to prioritize vocal display over realistic characterization. He began to experiment with ways of structuring scenes in a more fluid way, and we can see an increasingly through-composed approach to scenic structure in his late operas in particular (for a full definition of the term 'through-composed', see p. 31). Despite his ambitions to be innovative and to challenge much-loved conventions, Verdi remained a highly popular composer throughout his career. He could truly be credited with having transformed the Italian operatic genre, and his innovations would be influential upon those who followed him.

Verdi's first big success was his third opera, *Nabucco* (1842). At this time in his life, as the movement for Italian unification was growing, many of Verdi's operas had a covert or even an overt political theme (I will return to this topic in Chapter Three). By the 1850s, however, Verdi was becoming increasingly interested in exploring human passions and the workings of human psychology in extreme circumstances. During this decade, Verdi wrote a trio of operas that have gone on to become pillars of the operatic repertory: *Rigoletto* (1851), *Il trovatore* (1853) and *La traviata* (1853). The first and last of these reflect Verdi's new preoccupations particularly well. Both have central characters who are, in a sense, outsider figures: Rigoletto is a hunchbacked jester who is cruelly betrayed by his master, the philandering Duke of Mantua, while the heroine of *La traviata* is a courtesan, used by gentlemen for their own pleasure but ostracized when she attempts to join polite society.

La traviata also demonstrates the fact that Verdi began to turn to a variety of different types of literary source by mid career. This opera – a work in which Verdi demonstrated his growing interest in dramatic and musical realism – was based upon a very recent play, Alexandre Dumas's *La Dame aux camélias* (1852), which Dumas had adapted from his own autobiographical novel, written four years earlier. For the most part, however, Verdi and his librettists chose earlier sources, although these were eclectic in national origin. Some were drawn from the Romantic period, such as plays by Lord Byron (his *The Two Foscari* became Verdi's *I due Foscari*) and Victor Hugo (his *Hernani* and *Le Roi s'amuse* became *Ernani* (1844) and *Rigoletto* respectively). On several occasions, Verdi and his librettists looked back even further, to the works of Shakespeare: *Macbeth*, *Othello* (*Otello*) and *The*

Merry Wives of Windsor (*Falstaff*). Shakespeare's plays were little known in Italy before the nineteenth century and opera played an important role in introducing them to Italian audiences. The interpretations of Shakespearean plays by Verdi and his librettists were notably more faithful to the original works than some operas by earlier Italian composers had been. For instance Rossini's *Otello* (1816) was based on a mishmash of different versions of the Othello story and was only tangentially related to Shakespeare's play, with many crucial plot details being altered and the opera even sometimes being played (due to censorship restrictions) with a happy ending. Verdi's *Otello*, by contrast, has often been held up as a masterpiece to rival Shakespeare's original. By this time, Verdi's eye was set firmly on the future. He had abandoned the old Italian operatic conventions and was writing operas that were increasingly through-composed and harmonically adventurous, placing a premium upon new ways of achieving dramatic realism through music. One of Verdi's Shakespeare operas, *Macbeth*, exists in two versions, first performed in 1847 and 1865 respectively. This demonstrates Verdi's constant desire for self-renewal and to update his style, and several other of his operas also exist in multiple versions (for instance, *Simon Boccanegra*, premiered in two different versions in 1857 and 1881). Let's turn now to another composer who had his eye set firmly on the future.

Richard Wagner is an extremely important figure within the history of opera, the history of music more generally and, indeed, the history of nineteenth-century ideas. Some of the hallmarks of the German Romantic style and even of French Grand Opera can be detected in Wagner's early works, but he would soon go on to develop his own very distinctive approach to composing opera. Put simply, Wagner felt there was a 'crisis' in opera and went about developing radical ways of reinventing the art-form. Such was his hostility to the operatic world he saw around him that he did not even use the word 'opera' to describe his works, coining the term 'music drama' in its place. His music dramas were radically different – both musically and dramatically – from operas along the Italian or French lines, although his works would go on to influence composers in both those countries. Wagner also wrote many theoretical texts in which he explained his ideas about reinventing the operatic art-form.

Wagner's music dramas are on an epic scale in terms of duration, performing resources and subject matter. They typically last for between three and five hours (*Die Meistersinger von Nürnberg* (1868) lasts four hours and fifteen minutes, and *Parsifal* (1882) approaches four-and-a-half hours). The Ring (*Der Ring des Nibelungen*), meanwhile, is the biggest and most ambitious work ever written in the history of Western music. First performed complete in 1876, it consists of a cycle of four works that Wagner intended to be performed over three days and a preliminary evening: *Das Rheingold* (1869, two hours, thirty minutes), *Die Walküre* (1870, three hours, forty-five minutes), *Siegfried* (1876, four hours, fifteen minutes) and *Götterdämmerung* (1876, four hours, fifteen minutes). The works were written to be performed in a festival setting at a specially built theatre (the 'Festspielhaus') in Bayreuth, southern Germany. In this respect, Wagner, like the very earliest opera theorists, was harking back to the model of the Ancient Greeks: he hoped to recreate an event akin to the festival of Dionysus, which took place in ancient Athens.

The Festspielhaus was a totally new type of opera house. Wagner wanted to do away with the traditional, Italian-style opera house with its horseshoe shape and boxes, because this design meant that many audience members had a poor view of the stage. (Indeed, it harked from a time when audience members were just as interested in looking at their fellow audience members as they were at the action on stage.) Wagner replaced this design with a more democratic one in which all of the seats faced the stage and in which the view was equally good from all seats. (This design has been taken up in many twentieth-century theatres and cinemas.) Wagner also thought very carefully about other aspects of the theatrical experience in commissioning the Festspielhaus. He designed the theatre so that the orchestra was concealed in a pit and he lowered the house lights in order to focus the audience's attention completely upon the action on stage rather than upon what was going on in the auditorium. Another respect in which Wagner took control over opera – and made his works the product of a single man's vision – was in writing his own texts rather than working with a librettist. He also became involved in set design and direction. Thus, in Wagner's case we can see a very different approach to opera to the highly collaborative model that reigned supreme in earlier periods.

Wagner's works were strongly influenced by philosophical ideas. This can be seen particularly clearly in his work *Tristan und Isolde* (1865). The opera takes place in a Celtic setting during the Middle Ages, reflecting the nineteenth-century interest in this historical period. It is essentially a monument to the notion of an ideal love through which the characters are redeemed and united in death. Wagner stripped the literary sources for this work to their bare essentials: Tristan and Isolde dominate the proceedings and their emotional situation is prioritized above 'action' in the conventional sense. Tristan, a Breton nobleman, has travelled to Cornwall to visit his uncle, Marke, where he falls in love with Marke's betrothed, Isolde. Tristan will ultimately commit suicide in his despair, and Isolde will collapse, dead but 'transfigured', upon his body. Wagner wrote of his ambition to depict through music a passion that was so intense that its consummation could be experienced only through death. For Tristan and Isolde, the ideal climax to their relationship is that their souls should be united: their relationship is founded not so much on the physical as upon philosophical ideals.

At the time of writing this work, Wagner was heavily influenced by the ideas of the philosopher Schopenhauer, who formulated theories about what he called the 'will' – essentially the human drive for power, sex, even life itself. Schopenhauer regarded the will as fundamentally destructive, and called for the repression of desire. Thus Tristan and Isolde's relationship, though charged with eroticism, is essentially founded upon mysticism and a yearning for salvation in the afterlife. However, Wagner's personal circumstances also had a role to play in shaping this work. At the time of writing *Tristan und Isolde*, he was engaged in an intense and highly idealized relationship with Mathilde Wesendonck, the wife of his patron, who had allowed Wagner and his wife to live in a house upon his estate. Ultimately, Wagner and Mathilde were forced to abandon their relationship when their spouses found out about it: their own perpetual yearning was mirrored in *Tristan und Isolde* itself.

Wagner reinvented the musical language of opera. He moved away from the Italian style, in which the voice predominated, and placed greater emphasis upon the orchestra as the bearer of emotion and musical meaning. Wagner used an increasingly adventurous harmonic language: *Tristan und Isolde*, although first performed in the 1860s, is sometimes held up as the first 'modern' work of music, pointing the way forward to the dissonance (or harmonic instability) of early twentieth-century music. Wagner also abandoned the 'number' approach to constructing opera, in which operas were made up of discrete arias (linked by recitative) that could be lifted from the opera and performed independently, and in which the moments where the audience was expected to applaud were clearly signalled. Wagner's works, on the other hand, were increasingly 'through-composed', with the music flowing on continuously, melding arias and ensembles together seamlessly, and never stopping for applause. It is virtually impossible to extract an 'aria' as such from a Wagner opera, and he also gave the orchestra a much more important musical and dramatic role. A particularly strong influence upon Wagner was Beethoven – rather surprisingly, since Beethoven made only one foray into writing opera (*Fidelio*, 1805). Nevertheless, Wagner felt that there was much potential in incorporating a quasi-symphonic approach into the structure of his operas. Wagner sought to create 'unity' in his works through the use of motifs, in much the same way as Beethoven had done in his later symphonies.

Wagner wanted to go beyond the simple 'reminiscence' motifs that had been used in French, German and Italian operas to date. Reminiscence motifs are melodies that are attached to a particular character and which are heard again when that character appears on stage or when another character thinks about them. Although Wagner used this approach in his earlier works, he gradually developed a more subtle and sophisticated system of motifs, which could represent not only characters but objects or more abstract concepts or states of mind. The *Leitmotiv* system (as it has come to be called, although Wagner himself never used the term) was applied across a vast musical canvas in Wagner's Ring Cycle, and Wagner was radical not just in using a far more extensive number of motifs than other composers, but in the way in which he modified them in many subtle ways in order to demonstrate how a character or an idea had changed across the course of a work. Many music scholars from Wagner's time to the present have attempted to attach labels to the various motifs, but have been unable to agree conclusively upon a system, since the *Leitmotiv*s are so many and so complex and take on different meanings as the drama develops. All of Wagner's new approaches to musical drama would have a profound influence upon the operatic composers who followed him: the influence of his innovations can be seen in the works of composers as diverse as Richard Strauss, Giacomo Puccini and Vincent D'Indy.

Other nineteenth-century trends

In my discussion of nineteenth-century opera, I have concentrated primarily upon two composers whose careers spanned many decades of the century, who took opera in radical new directions, and whose works are still considered to be central to the operatic canon today. However, nineteenth-century opera was extremely diverse, particularly in the later part of the century, and we might point to numerous other composers from this period whose careers and works are equally interesting. In late nineteenth-century France, operas flourished at the hands of composers including Bizet, Delibes and Massenet. These composers, like many painters of their day, were particularly drawn to 'exotic' settings – Delibes's *Lakmé* (1883) is set in India, Bizet's *Les Pêcheurs des perles* ('The Pearl Fishers', 1863) in Ceylon (now Sri Lanka) and the same composer's *Carmen* (1875) in a strikingly 'orientalized' Spain, while Massenet's *Thaïs* (1894) is set in Coptic Egypt. This question of operatic exoticism will be addressed in more detail in Chapter Four. Other French composers such as Emmanuel Chabrier, Vincent D'Indy and Ernest Chausson, whose operatic works are less well remembered today, embarked upon a rather different course. They were strongly influenced by Wagnerian techniques (including through-composition, the use of *Leitmotivs* and a prominent role for the orchestra), often drawing upon mythology or setting their works in Celtic locations. Unsurprisingly, many German composers of this period also took their lead from Wagner.

However, it is important to remember that opera also flourished during the nineteenth century in places other than the traditional operatic centres of Italy, France and the German-speaking lands which I have prioritized here. The first indigenous Russian operas were written in the late eighteenth century and particularly notable nineteenth-century opera composers from Russia include

Glinka, Tchaikovsky, Mussorgsky, Rimsky-Korsakov and others. Such composers often drew upon their rich heritage of native literature: Glinka's *Ruslan and Lyudmila* (1842) was based upon an adaptation of a Pushkin poem, as was Tchaikovsky's *Eugene Onegin* (1879). Some operas by Russian composers could be said to be relatively 'Western' in musical language; others bear the distinctive hallmark of Russian folk music in their melodic, harmonic and phrasal structures, and many Russian operas are based on subjects that deal with distinctly Russian preoccupations or episodes from Russian history.

As part of a general drift towards musical nationalism in the later decades of the nineteenth century, composers in many other parts of Europe began to use opera as a way of exploring and asserting their national identity, often looking to regional folk legends for inspiration. Here we might point, for instance, to the Czech operas of composers such as Bedřich Smetana and Antonin Dvořák. Indigenous operatic genres also flourished in countries including Romania, Hungary, Yugoslavia, Greece, Spain and the Scandinavian lands. In Britain, where foreign operas were regularly performed, there were calls for a national school of opera to be established. One of the more successful British operas of the nineteenth century was *The Bohemian Girl* (1843) by the composer Michael Balfe (who was born in Ireland but made his home in England). There was a flourishing of English operas during the later nineteenth century (including a large number of Wagner-inspired works), but very few of these achieved any sort of lasting success, apart from comic works. The vastly popular operettas of Gilbert and Sullivan, written between 1875 and 1896, parodied serious opera as much as they satirized British social conventions, but not even Sullivan found success when he tried his hand at writing an English 'Grand Opera' (*Ivanhoe*, 1891). The British would have to wait until the next century to achieve genuinely international success in the operatic field.

The eclectic twentieth century

More and more diverse styles of opera developed in different countries during the twentieth century, making it even more difficult to make generalizations about twentieth-century operas than about those of the nineteenth. At the same time, we might point to a decline in the traditional, Italian model of opera during the twentieth century. By the end of the nineteenth century there was some sense that opera was not flourishing to the extent that it once had as a creative art-form. Whereas in the eighteenth century most operas that were performed were new, there was now a fully established repertory system, meaning that popular operas were performed again and again, and fewer new works were being written. Partly the reasons for this were economic, but they also stemmed from the fact that composers were ever keener to put a highly individual stamp upon each work. To a certain extent, economic limitations such as the decline of traditional aristocratic patronage have made opera a prohibitively expensive art-form in the modern age. Composers still write operas today, but it would be rare to find a contemporary composer writing a three- or four-hour opera with lavish scenery, a large cast and full orchestra, as many nineteenth-century composers did. However, the reasons for the changes in opera in the twentieth century have been aesthetic, ideological even, as well as simply pragmatic. Many twentieth-century composers have deliberately turned away from what they have seen as the 'excesses' of opera in previous centuries, choosing to write chamber operas instead, or to experiment with different ways of creating drama through music. However, before we examine these later developments, let's return to the very beginning of the twentieth century, and to the works which might be said to form a bridge between the nineteenth and twentieth centuries.

A movement developed in Italy around 1890 known as *Verismo*, or realist opera, which continued into the early twenti-

CREATING DRAMA THROUGH MUSIC

Just like a play or a film, an opera needs to create drama. It must feature a compelling narrative and appealing characters and build in moments of tension and climax. However, an opera has certain advantages over a play or a film in the resources at its disposal. Opera uses music not just as an atmosphere-creating device in the background (as would be the case with a film soundtrack) but as an incredibly powerful dramatic tool in its own right. In an opera, music can be used in subtle ways to convey messages to the audience that could not be conveyed by text alone. For instance, if a playwright wishes to signal that a character is lying, he or she can demonstrate this to the audience only through visual means – the character's gestures, facial expression and general demeanour. The opera composer has an additional medium of dramatic significa-tion at his or her disposal: music can be used to contradict the text, by conjuring up a mood, for instance, which is at odds with the words a character is singing. Music can also be combined with text in clever ways in an opera in order to demonstrate either conflict or union between characters.

eth century: key figures in this movement were Mascagni, Leoncavallo, Cilea and Giordano. There had been earlier attempts to create social 'realism' in opera – obvious examples include Verdi's *La traviata* or Bizet's *Carmen* – but the *Verismo* movement took things one step further. These works dealt with ordinary characters, sometimes drawn from what one might call society's 'low-life' and they often depicted situations that were violent, gritty or seedy. Giordano's *La mala vita* (literally 'the bad life', 1892), for instance, portrayed the world of Neapolitan prostitutes. The libretti for such operas were usually drawn from the *Verismo* school of Italian literature, often the short stories of Sicilian writer Giovanni Verga. The subject matter of these works was usually matched by a music that was suitably violent, moving away from the emphasis on lyricism so important in earlier Italian opera and at times blending singing with shouting; nevertheless, these operas often still included impassioned 'number' arias that could be detached from the opera and, crucially, recorded. Enrico Caruso was the first opera singer to make a fortune from recordings, at the beginning of the twentieth century, and many of his records were of *Verismo* arias.

A high proportion of the *Verismo* operas were one-act works. Sometimes the reason for this was pragmatic – for instance, Mascagni's *Cavalleria rusticana* (1890), one of the most famous *Verismo* works, was written in response to a competition run by the music publisher Sonzogno inviting young composers to write one-act operas. Nevertheless, the one-act format was ideal for the *Verismo* genre in many respects, allowing composers to create a new and exciting way of telling a story through music. Whereas a long opera can depict the events of an entire lifetime, a short opera had to hit you right between the eyes, with no scope for complicated subplots, secondary characters, emotional subtlety or protracted romances – perfect for the rather crude, brutal world of *Verismo*. The composer had to create his situation in a few broad brushstrokes, giving a snapshot of a particular time and place. This almost photographic quality made the short opera an effective way of turning the spotlight onto the everyday. But if the proportions of *Verismo* operas were small, the passions they portrayed were larger than life. Like a newspaper story, the short opera must get straight to the point and hurtle rapidly towards its conclusion, so one-act *Verismo* operas concentrate less on the sentimental and more on the sensational. Love is presented in its most blunt and extreme forms: lust, jealousy and betrayal. Composers in other countries around this time also attempted to depict realistic situations, also often depicting the poorest members of society. A good example is Gustave Charpentier's *Louise* (1900), set in the Montmartre district of Paris, about a struggle between a young girl drawn to the Bohemian lifestyle and her working-class parents. However, few composers outside of Italy achieved the raw emotion and lyrical passion that was so distinctive of the *Verismo* style.

A composer sometimes associated with the *Verismo* movement is Giacomo Puccini, although in fact most of his works (with the possible exceptions of *Tosca* (1900) and *Il tabarro* (1918)) technically stand apart from that tradition. Together with the operas of Verdi, Puccini's works are probably among those most frequently performed in opera houses today. Puccini was depicted during his lifetime as the much-wanted 'successor to Verdi', but in fact he would develop a style of opera that was very much his own. His career straddled the period between the 1880s and the 1920s and although his operas bear some hallmarks of the Italian tradition − notably, a striking gift for melody − they also bear the influence of some of the more experimental developments in pan-European modern music. His works are more through-composed than most nineteenth-century Italian operas and Wagner was certainly an influence (although Puccini never entirely abandoned the idea of the detachable 'number'), but so too were composers as diverse as Debussy and Stravinsky. Puccini's last opera, *Turandot* (left unfinished at his death in 1924; premiered in 1926 with an ending by Franco Alfano), sums up some of these apparent contradictions. It uses a very 'modern' and at times dissonant musical language, and its movement flows on relatively seamlessly and naturally, yet the opera contains one of the best-known arias to have been regularly performed independently of its operatic context − 'Nessun Dorma', used most famously in the UK as the theme song of the 1990 World Cup soccer tournament.

Puccini regarded himself quintessentially as a 'man of the theatre' and was attentive to the dramatic details of his works, creating believable characters and human situations wherever his works were set, whether this be Renaissance Florence, Gold Rush America or early twentieth-century Japan. His capacity for empathy, arguably bordering on sentimentality, and his formula for creating a guaranteed tear-jerker, is what has endeared his works to audiences the world over, although it is precisely these same qualities that have long made scholars suspicious and critical of his works. If Puccini was the successor to Verdi – and this is a moot point because we could point to many stylistic differences between their works – he himself was to have no heir. The great tradition of lyrical Italian opera is often said to have come to a (very passionate) conclusion with Puccini: *Turandot* was essentially the last Italian opera to gain an uncontested place in the mainstream operatic repertory. Italian composers continued to write operas, but figures such as Malipiero, Pizzetti and Casella did not achieve Puccini's popular international success; indeed, they did not seek to do so. Those composers who saw themselves as modernists realized that their artistic aims were at odds with the Italian operatic tradition, a tradition in which popular approval and instant emotional appeal were essential criteria for a work's success, and to varying degrees they rejected the expressive conventions of the nineteenth-century operatic tradition.

Composers elsewhere, working in different traditions or, indeed, creating new schools of national opera, were not faced with the same problem of having to continue a tradition so strongly steeped in lyricism, tonality and human sentiment. Such freedom allowed them to reconcile opera and modern music more easily, to use the opera house as a forum for experiment. Elsewhere in Europe, opera was becoming more and more diverse. In France, for example, Debussy brought together opera and literary symbolism in his opera *Pelléas et Mélisande* (1902, based on a play written nine years earlier by Maurice Maeterlinck), turning his back altogether upon the contemporary trend for operatic realism. *Pelléas* is largely through-composed and owes much to Wagner, but Debussy developed a style of word-setting in this opera that mimicked the gently flowing patterns of spoken French. Indeed, he allowed the text to prevail over the music, and avoided passages of lyricism in the Italian sense, allowing the music to predominate only in the orchestral preludes and interludes. *Pelléas* is also a work in which the drama is subtle, spiritual and mysterious almost to the point of being vague: we are worlds away here from the forceful expression and overstated sentimentality of the contemporary *Verismo* works.

In 1900s Germany, meanwhile, Richard Strauss was experimenting in his operas *Salome* (1905) and *Elektra* (1909) with what might be termed a 'decadent' operatic aesthetic, preoccupied with grotesque elements of sexuality. *Salome*, based upon Oscar Wilde's play (1896), recounts the New Testament story of King Herod's lust for his step-daughter Salome and hers in turn for the prophet Jochanaan (John the Baptist), who has been imprisoned in the royal palace. Herod asks Salome to dance for him and in return will give her whatever she desires: she asks for the prophet's head on a silver platter, which she then proceeds to kiss. With its themes of incest and necrophilia, and the fact that it featured the first operatic strip-tease (the 'dance of the seven veils'), *Salome* caused a sensation. It was banned in Vienna for over a decade, and in London was performed in German, without an English translation or even a plot summary, until the 1930s. Yet despite its capacity to shock and offend, *Salome* was immensely popular with audiences; indeed, Strauss was able to build a house with the profits he made from this opera.

Strauss matched his daring subject matter with new approaches to composition. *Salome* is almost 'symphonic' in its approach, akin to a tone poem with words. The one-act format, with no let-up in the music for almost two hours, and the relentless chromaticism created a fevered, stifling atmosphere that was highly appropriate for the opera's theme of obsession. Strauss's sumptuous orchestration was the perfect match for Wilde's lavishly decorative prose and for the 'decadent' themes brought out in the libretto: intoxication, heightened senses, exoticism, sadism, vivid colours and details. Wagner was clearly an influence, once again, not only upon Strauss's prominent use of the orchestra but upon his harmonic language (a leaning towards dissonance) and his system of motifs. Works such as *Salome* had something in common with Debussy's *Pelléas et Mélisande* in that both were based on prose rather than verse libretti: the irregular musical phrases such composers employed meant that a libretto composed of regular rhyme schemes was no longer necessary. Thus it became increasingly possible for composers to set plays pretty much as they stood, albeit with some cuts to accommodate the fact that dialogue is conveyed more slowly when it is sung than when it is spoken.

More radical approaches to opera were afoot elsewhere. It may seem somewhat surprising that Arnold Schoenberg, the leader of the modernist movement, should have written operas, as opera was by and large disparaged by the modernists as pandering to the sentimental desires of the bourgeoisie. But Schoenberg's operas were nothing like anything that had ever been heard on the operatic stage before. His Expressionist opera *Erwartung* ('Expectation') is a work with a single character – a nameless woman, who is wandering in a forest, looking for her lover, whom she eventually finds dead underneath a bench – and is more about atmosphere than action. Schoenberg is clearly not concerned here with dramatic interaction, nor really with character development. Rather, this is an opera almost entirely concerned with the workings of the subconscious: Schoenberg doesn't make it clear whether the drama is real or simply the product of the woman's angst-ridden imagination. He wrote *Erwartung* in Vienna in 1909 (although it was not performed until 1924), where everybody was talking about the radical ideas of Sigmund Freud. The nightmare world of the opera is clearly influenced by Freud's theory that dreams represent our hidden anxieties and desires, and the trauma that the lone character experiences is matched by suitably dissonant, yet dramatic, music. Many other early twentieth-century composers would take a similar interest in the workings of the human psyche and in the unconscious: one might also point to such strikingly modern operas as Bartók's *Duke Bluebeard's Castle* (1918) and Berg's *Wozzeck* (1925) and *Lulu* (1937).

Like *Salome*, *Erwartung* is a one-act opera and again the format suited the dramatic material: the lack of an interval meant that the audience was held captive, forced to share the paranoia of the character on stage. But the performing forces of *Erwartung* were vastly pared down in comparison to *Salome*, with its sumptuous, expanded orchestration, and Schoenberg set a trend for chamber operas that influenced many experimental twentieth-century composers. In part this turn towards short operas was an inevitable backlash against the monumentality of nineteenth-century opera. Furthermore, it demonstrated the modernists' contempt for the 'social' aspects of opera that Wagner had also lamented. The lack of an interval forced audiences to listen more carefully, to focus their attention upon the music and the action on stage. Although opera-going had become a more serious business in the nineteenth century than it had been in the eighteenth, a trip to the opera was still primarily a social occasion: a chance to catch up with the gossip and parade your best dress. By cutting out the intervals, twentieth-century opera composers forced the audience's attention back onto the opera itself.

One might counterpoint the more experimental approach of composers such as Schoenberg and Berg with a branch of operatic 'neoclassicism' during the mid twentieth century, as represented by works such as Stravinsky's *The Rake's Progress* (1951). In such works, Stravinsky made a conscious return to tonality (indeed, he borrows consciously from the musical idioms of the eighteenth and nineteenth centuries) and to operatic 'numbers'. Despite effectively 'looking backwards', Stravinsky brought experiment to the operatic genre in other ways: *Oedipus Rex* (1927), for instance, was innovative in combining opera with aspects of oratorio and in calling for its characters to wear masks as a deliberately alienating device.

As the twentieth century progressed, composers explored increasingly divergent approaches to operatic composition. It is difficult to write a history of twentieth-century opera in terms of 'schools' or broad tendencies: instead we have to view the history of twentieth-century opera as having been governed by a spirit of individual experimentation. As I've noted above, one of the striking developments in twentieth-century opera is its vast geographical spread. Operas continued to be written in Italy, France and Germany (even if national traditions were being challenged), but we also find twentieth-century opera flourishing in Russia, Eastern Europe (famously, for example, the nationalist works of Czech composer Leoš Janáček), Scandinavia (for instance the Danish composer Carl Nielsen) and the Iberian peninsula. Some of these had also been flourishing centres in the nineteenth century. However, it would be reasonable to say that Britain and the USA developed into new centres for operatic composition only in the twentieth century. As we have seen, despite the experiments in music theatre by Purcell in the seventeenth century, and the popularity of Italian opera in London from the eighteenth century (and German and French opera by the nineteenth), opera as a national art-form did not really take off in Britain as it had in other countries. Opera (and, to some extent, music per se) was regarded as an occupation for foreigners: in a book on English opera published in 1911, Cecil Forsyth crudely and chauvinistically argued that although Italians were good at writing operas they were no good at fighting wars, whereas the reverse applied to the British. There was a concerted attempt during the early twentieth century by composers including Charles Villiers Stanford, Rutland Boughton and Ethel Smyth to create a school of English opera, but few works from this period managed to establish a firm foothold in the repertory. However, a more successful school of English opera developed in the mid twentieth century, as composers including Benjamin Britten, Michael Tippett and William Walton embraced the form.

Britten, probably the most successful of the three, wrote incidental music as a young man for theatre, film and radio, which proved an excellent training ground for his later operatic works. He was interested in the formal problems posed by opera composition in the twentieth century – how to deal with the question of operatic 'numbers' and how to respond to the Wagnerian inheritance. He was also preoccupied by the idea of using the operatic form to confront social injustice and intolerance, an endeavour shaped by his own experiences as a homosexual and a pacifist. Thus, his operas often feature an 'outsider' figure of some form or another: *Peter Grimes* (1945), for instance, treats the subject of a Suffolk fisherman who is ostracised by local villagers when his young apprentices are found dead in suspicious circumstances. Another notable feature of Britten's operas is the fact that many were deeply imbued with a conscious spirit of Englishness: this is reflected both in their subject matter and in their use of a folk-song-inflected musical language. The school of British opera could be said to be still flourishing today: new works by composers such as Harrison Birtwistle or Thomas Adès are performed with reasonable regularity at prestigious theatres such as the Royal Opera House in London.

American opera is very much a phenomenon of the twentieth century, although European operas had been at the heart of the social scene for wealthy Americans for much of the nineteenth century. American operas have been strikingly diverse and influenced by non-operatic musical genres: one might point in particular to works influenced by the Broadway musical, such as George Gershwin's *Porgy and Bess* (1935) and some of the works of Leonard Bernstein such as *Candide* (1956). Works like these raise interesting questions about what constitutes an opera, as opposed to a work of musical theatre. At the other end of the spectrum, some American composers have been as interested in experiment as their European counterparts (one might point to the avant-garde works of composers such as Roger Sessions). However, some of the later twentieth-century American composers have managed to strike a balance between novelty and box office success – minimalist operas by composers such as Philip Glass, for instance, have found a wide audience. American composers have also continued the long-standing tradition of opera composers engaging with the political issues of the day. A particularly striking example would be John Adams, with works including *Nixon in China* (1985–7) and *The Death of Klinghoffer* (1991) (see Chapter Three). American opera has also been particularly varied because of the ethnic diversity of its nation's citizenship. In the mid twentieth century, the USA benefited musically from the presence of a number of composers exiled from Nazi Germany such as Kurt Weill. By the late twentieth century, meanwhile, Asian–American and Chinese composers resident in America (such as Tan Dun) were beginning to attract attention on the operatic stage.

There has been much discussion in recent years about the 'death of opera'. As we have already seen, opera in the twentieth century has faced financial challenges: traditional forms of patronage have died out, and operas are increasingly expensive to stage. Furthermore, the theory that opera has burned itself out may also stem from the idea that many opera houses today could be said to be perpetuating what we might call a musical 'museum culture'. That is to say, the repertories of most opera houses today tend to be based upon a core selection of works drawn from the late eighteenth to the early twentieth centuries. The experience of the typical contemporary opera-goer is very different from that of audiences in previous centuries: the modern opera-goer may watch endless repetitions of the same canon of much-loved works, whereas their predecessors from earlier centuries would have, by and large, been treated to an ever-changing diet of new operas. This has undoubtedly changed the operatic experience, the ways in which we respond to opera as an art-form and its place in contemporary society. One might even say that audiences have become suspicious of operas written during their own lifetime, fearing that composers have pushed the boundaries so far as to make their works completely inaccessible. It would be true to say that some operatic composers in recent years may have felt that their role is to push artistic boundaries rather than to satisfy audience demand to the extent expected of composers in the past. But audiences too have perhaps become more timid, preferring to stick to a small repertory of tried and tested favourites than to experience something new.

Nevertheless, accusations that opera is dead are certainly exaggerated. Composers today continue to find opera a stimulating genre in which to compose, however far they may have diverged from its traditional forms and conventions. And while staging modern operas can undoubtedly be financially risky, larger opera houses are still willing and able to take that risk, using sell-out productions of *Le nozze di Figaro* or *La bohème* to 'subsidize' more challenging operas, lesser-known works or operas by up-and-coming composers, which are often performed in chamber productions or in studio theatres rather than in the main auditorium. The less lavish scale of many recent operas means that they lend themselves better to performance in such spaces; indeed, some composers have experimented with writing operas that will not be performed in opera houses at all, but in a variety of public spaces. Opera today, then, could be said to fall into two categories: on the one hand, a rarely changing 'canon' of old favourites, and on the other, works which are bold and eclectic and which continue to confront society's expectations. For all the talk of opera being dead, composers are showing no signs of giving up just yet on this infinitely flexible way of representing human experience through music and words.

2
Opera on and offstage

The rest of this book examines the various critical and interpretative approaches that have been taken towards opera in recent decades. As I have already mentioned in the Introduction, scholars are now to some degree less interested in musical works as 'texts' than they were in the past. New avenues of enquiry have opened up within musicology more broadly that examine the ways in which musical works are performed and received, shifting the focus of study onto the interpreter – and indeed the audience – as much as the composer. (There is also greater recognition today of the fact that many operas from the past were created collaboratively by large groups of people rather than simply by a composer and librettist.) It is therefore inevitable that performance and production issues should have come to preoccupy opera scholars in recent years. The sorts of issues that interest them include not only the practical processes a theatre has to go through to put on an opera but the ideologies and politics of updating opera productions to reflect contemporary concerns.

Discussions to do with production issues have become even more intriguing as operas have started to be performed in an ever-growing number of venues outside the traditional opera house, something I will discuss later on in this chapter. Furthermore, scholars have recently started to take an interest in the numerous films that have been made of operas, whether filmed theatrical performances or performances conceived especially for film, with the additional scenic possibilities film technology permits. Scholars have asked questions about the ways in which operas have been altered to suit the medium of film, the ways in which film can enhance or diminish the operatic experience, and whether opera on film ought perhaps to be regarded as a genre or art-form in its own right. This chapter introduces you to some of the key debates that have taken place in these areas.

The process of bringing an opera to the stage is a long and complicated one, involving decisions and preparations that typically take many years. The choice of opera has to be balanced alongside other works in the same and in recent seasons; often theatres will aim to put on a contrasting range of works in a given season, in terms of historical period, national-ity and subject matter. If a new or lesser-known work is to be staged, the theatre will often offset the financial risk incurred by putting on a popular opera in the same season that is guaranteed to 'balance the books'. (For instance, at the time I'm writing this book, the San Francisco Opera's current season includes peren-nial favourites such as Puccini's *La bohème* and Verdi's *La travi-ata*, but also a number of more unusual or adventurous works, including Erich Korngold's *Die Tote Stadt* (*The Dead City*, 1920), and *The Bonesetter's Daughter* (2008), adapted as a libretto by Amy Tan from her own novel and set to music by contem-porary American composer Stewart Wallace.) A large creative team is involved in planning a new production of an opera, and will have to balance the preferences and artistic vision of the conductor, director, designer and perhaps even the lead singers (although singers have less clout in dictating their fellow cast members than the most powerful did in the seventeenth and eighteenth centuries). Assembling a cast can be a complicated business, as singers are usually booked up several years ahead: this is obviously of particular concern to wealthy international opera houses, such as the Metropolitan Opera in New York, which seek to book the most prestigious stars from across the world. Other opera companies, on the other hand, may draw upon a group of 'repertory' singers, whom they employ on a regular basis.

The business of casting is also more complicated today because contemporary critics and audiences increasingly go to operas with the expectation that they will be visually believable as well as vocally impressive. In earlier decades and centuries, dramatic credibility was sometimes deemed less important than a beautiful voice – here I'd point to the example of Nellie Melba singing the role of Mimì in *La bohème* (a character surely intended to be in her early twenties at most) well into her sixties at the beginning of the twentieth century. Even further back in history, in the eighteenth century, 'dramatic realism', as we understand it today, was not regarded as something to which opera singers were expected to strive. A principal singer would strike a pose and deliver an aria directly to the audience. There was a complex language of physical gestures used by singers then and during the nineteenth century that audiences today would find unfamiliar and perhaps difficult to understand.

Today – for better or worse – audiences expect their opera singers to be as credible and visually alluring as film stars. This growing tendency to place a premium on the visual aspects of opera casting was exemplified recently by the much-publicized sacking of the soprano Deborah Voigt from a production of Richard Strauss's *Ariadne auf Naxos* (1916) at the Royal Opera House in London in 2004 because she was unable to fit into the little black dress that the designer deemed essential to his conception of the leading role. Audiences (not to mention directors) also expect opera singers today to act as convincingly as film stars – at least when performing operas from the nineteenth century onwards – whereas in the mid twentieth century it was more acceptable for star singers simply to 'stand and sing'.

THE PRIMA DONNA

The *prima donna* has been a celebrated figure since opera's earliest beginnings. The lead soprano is often given the largest role and the most demanding music in an opera, and typically receives the most applause at the end. An image of excess has been constructed around *prima donnas* in the popular imagination – they are seen as glamorous yet also extravagant, self-centred and demanding – with the consequence that they have sometimes been reviled as well as adored. Indeed, the phrase 'prima donna' has entered common usage, denoting someone who acts in a spoiled and capricious manner. Some leading ladies have consciously cultivated airs and graces whilst others have distanced themselves from the *prima donna* clichés, wishing only to be admired as hard-working professionals. But we might argue that not all leading ladies necessarily qualify for 'prima donna' status. Taken positively, the word is reserved for those who offer something beyond the norm – not just a unique voice but mesmerising acting, a magnetic personality and striking looks. The Greek soprano Maria Callas possessed all of these qualities and is seen as perhaps the archetypal *prima donna* of the twentieth century. Time will tell which of today's leading sopranos are granted such recognition by posterity.

Nevertheless, it would be misguided of us to assume that opera productions today are necessarily visually and dramatically more sophisticated than they were in past centuries. The production books that the Ricordi publishing house put together for the early performances of some of Verdi's later operas demonstrate that Verdi was extremely interested in guiding every dramatic nuance of his works (I shall return to discussing these books later in this chapter). Staging practices have varied greatly throughout the history of opera and in different parts of the world. Only where historical documents have come to light is it possible for us to express any sort of informed opinion about staging issues and performance practice from the past, and even then written descriptions of performances or even illustrations are limited in what they can tell us about aspects of performance such as gesture, facial expression or what singers from past centuries actually sounded like.

If it is difficult to find out about styles of performance practice from earlier centuries, it is much easier to gain access to the visual side of opera productions from the past – what the scenery and costumes looked like – because so many illustrations have survived. (Whether we would want to use this information to 'recreate' the look of stagings from the past is another issue, which I shall discuss in more detail presently.) From the earliest days of opera, visual display was important – remember that the earliest Italian operas were often commissioned for one noble-man to impress his political rivals, so lavish scenery and costumes were effectively a conscious display of wealth and power. Stage designers from the seventeenth and eighteenth centuries produced sets that were as lavish as palaces, often using clever *trompe l'oeil* effects (an optical illusion that made a backdrop appear three dimensional) to astonish and impress the audience members. A particularly innovative set designer of the seven-teenth century was Giacomo Torelli, who worked during the 1640s at the Teatro Novissimo in Venice and subsequently in France: his major achievement was in creating a realistic sense of perspective, creating sets that were not 'flat' but which seemed to extend backwards into infinity. From its very beginnings in the seventeenth century, opera was also at the forefront of technological developments. The best-equipped opera houses had clever theatrical machinery that could be used not only to change sets in an instant but also to achieve seemingly magical or superhuman effects before the very eyes of the audience. Characters could, for instance, be flown around the stage: the action on stage could potentially mirror the vocal gymnastics of the principal singers.

However, the history of operatic staging has not always been one of visual excess. At various times in opera's history, composers have held different attitudes towards the staging of their works. Sometimes, as above, the emphasis has been upon creating visual spectacle for its own sake – either as a show of wealth or a display of theatrical illusion. At other times composers and librettists have called for scenic naturalism to match the dramatic realism that they are striving for in their works. At other times still, the tendency has moved more towards scenic abstraction. This has often tended to be the case in the twentieth century, although you can still see fairly lavish productions of traditional operas. The motivation for putting on a more pared-down production has sometimes been cost driven: some theatres simply cannot afford extravagant costumes and elaborate sets that are different for each act of an opera. Sometimes, however, the reasons for staging minimalist productions have been aesthetic rather than pragmatic. In the twentieth century a number of opera directors wished to move away from the nineteenth-century desire for realism to something more abstract, focusing the audience's attention away from the scenery and on to the performers and the opera itself.

In some cases operas have been conceived for specific theatres. Most notably, as discussed in Chapter One, Richard Wagner commissioned his own opera house, the Festspielhaus, to be built in the small Bavarian town of Bayreuth. After many years of planning (and much discussion of the relationship between aesthetics and physical space in his philosophical works), the theatre eventually opened its doors in 1876. Wagner was involved in the design of the theatre to a highly unusual degree, commissioning a theatrical space that would serve his art-works and within which the audience could focus upon his operas without distraction from their fellow audience members, from the orchestra (concealed in a pit) or from mechanical changes of scenery taking place before their eyes. *Parsifal* was the first opera to be written expressly for the new theatre and made the most of all of the theatre's particular properties. In an instance such as this, in which a composer has had such a controlling hand over the visual aspects of an opera, one might ask whether contemporary directors should feel obliged to attempt to recreate the composer's original vision. However, productions of Wagner's operas have in no sense become frozen in time; indeed, some of the most modern operatic stagings have been of Wagner's works. As early as the 1890s, Adolphe Appia was designing pared-down stagings of Wagner's works at Bayreuth. These productions used visual simplicity and placed emphasis upon lighting rather than two-dimensional sets as a way of creating scenic depth. After the Second World War, Wagner's grandson Wieland Wagner was yet more experimental at Bayreuth, doing away with pictorial sets and instead creating stagings based upon abstract symbolism.

Few if any other composers throughout history have had the opportunity to design their own theatrical space, ideally suited to their operas: most have tailored their operas to take account of the physical and technical capabilities of a given theatre. In nineteenth-century Italy, composers wrote operas with the expectation that they would be performed in different theatres around the country or even exported abroad. Nevertheless, these composers still sometimes worked closely with the designer at the original theatre, crafting their ideal scenery. For example, whenever Verdi was writing an opera for the Gran Teatro la Fenice in Venice, he would work closely with a designer called Giuseppe Bertoja. In total, the two men worked together on eight operas (including such famous works as *Rigoletto* and *La traviata*): composers of this period rarely worked with an individual designer so frequently. The two men built up a close working relationship which meant that Verdi could rely upon Bertoja to successfully translate his visual conception of an opera onto the stage. Perhaps you will find it surprising to learn that composers from the past had such strong views about what their operas should look like (as well as sound like). This raises interesting questions about how directors should interpret such operas today – I shall discuss this issue in the next section. As we shall see, debates about operatic staging today are often highly charged.

Issues that face producers and directors

Producers and directors today are faced by a number of challenges. Firstly, they need to think about how operas from the past – and in some cases what may seem to be a very distant past – can be made interesting to a modern audience. Should we attempt to transport operas into our contemporary world, or should we enter into the spirit of the composer's own time and possibly even seek to recreate an opera's original performance conditions? The issue of whether to update operas or not has become a controversial one in recent years.

Some might respond with hostility to the idea that it is necessary to update operas from the past to the spirit of our own age in order to maintain a contemporary audience's interest. If an opera has stood the test of time, one might argue, it must by definition deal with subjects that are timeless, express a message that is universal, and be intrinsically appealing enough in its music to be able to speak to a modern audience on its own terms. To assume that all works must by default be updated for modern audiences not only runs the risk of distorting the composer's conception of the work but is also potentially insult-ing to contemporary audiences, suggesting that they are incapable of understanding art-works unless they are made 'relevant' to their day-to-day lives. Indeed, many opera-goers today, as in the past, go to the theatre as a form of escapism. For some people experiencing opera for the first time, grand, historic costumes and sets may be what they imagine opera to be about – stark, pared-down staging and contemporary costumes can sometimes come as a disappointment.

Matters get more complicated if we start to take a purist line and talk about preserving and respecting a composer's original intentions. The question of 'authentic performance' has been a topic of intense debate in musicological circles over the past few decades. In the second half of the twentieth century, there was a trend towards 'period performance' (something that only a very few performers had thought about before that time), with many ensembles forming especially to perform a particular repertory in an historically informed manner. Scholars in turn began to debate the merits of period performance, asking questions about whether performers might have some sort of moral obligation to respect the composer's original intentions, and about the extent to which the available historical evidence made such an endeavour possible. Although the historically informed performance movement has been particularly strong in choral and instrumental music, there is no reason why we should not ask similar questions about the performance of opera. Here too, as with any other repertory, the question of historical evidence looms large, but there are even more factors to take into consideration which potentially complicate matters. How can we know what a composer and librettist intended, never mind the intentions of a director, designer or choreographer, and how ought we to prioritize the respective preferences of these various members of the original creative team?

In one particularly notable case, however, the evidence does exist to create a historically informed production, should a director wish to. In the later part of his career, Giuseppe Verdi, together with his publishing house Ricordi, put together production books or stage manuals, known as *disposizioni sceniche* (*disposizione scenica* in the singular), to outline precisely how the opera in question was staged in its first production. For many nineteenth-century operatic productions, illustrations survive of the original costumes and sets, but Verdi's highly detailed production books went several stages further. They include diagrams of the stage as viewed from above, using symbols to show precisely where singers stood, how they moved across the stage and even, in some cases, the arm gestures they made. The books are, in effect, rather similar to the books of dance notation that preserve the original choreography for ballets such as *Swan Lake*, which allow dancers today to recreate the steps used by their nineteenth-century predecessors. Verdi supplemented the illustrations with a written commentary, describing the facial expression a principal character should adopt or explaining precisely how a chorus should stand. (He often expressed a particular concern that the chorus members should not be 'wooden' in the way they moved and acted, suggesting that the choruses in many contemporary productions were just that!)

Furthermore, at least towards the end of Verdi's career, we know that the staging books were intended to be used as a model for future performances: Ricordi rented them out so that other theatres could recreate the performance conditions of the premiere. The fact that these books were produced indicates that Verdi had fairly strong feelings about the staging of his works: their existence seems to suggest that, in his eyes, there was a single correct or authoritative version of his operas. We might surmise that each book acted, in effect, as a guideline for an 'ideal' production. But we must also bear in mind the possibility that the motivation for producing the manuals was commercially as well as ideologically driven. As the Ricordi firm owned the commercial rights to the costumes that had to be used in subsequent productions, it is no wonder that the staging manuals cautioned theatres strongly against the use of any alternative costumes or props.

The staging manuals are fascinating as historical documents, giving us a glimpse of productions that were sanctioned by

Verdi himself and telling us much about nineteenth-century staging practices. Furthermore, they would in theory make it possible for a modern director to stage a performance that was fairly close, visually at least, to what Verdi and his audiences would have experienced. To do so would certainly be interesting and would allow us to feel that we were being given a glimpse into the past. However, the question of whether we ought to feel morally obliged to do so is a thornier one. One might suggest that in distributing the staging manuals to other theatres, Verdi and his publishers intended the original staging, costumes and movements to be maintained and that this is something that we ought to respect today. However, we could also point to a whole range of potential problems with this theory or reasons why such an approach could be limiting. We don't know for sure whether the original staging was actually Verdi's 'ideal' staging, in fact, or merely the best possible version given the local resources and personnel available to him.

Slavishly following the staging manuals would also do away with any sense of spontaneity: to put it bluntly, it would become rather dull if every production of *Otello*, whether it were staged in New York, Aix-en-Provence or Sydney, looked exactly the same. The idea of having one, fixed approach to staging an opera seems limiting to us today. The reason for this may be that fewer new works are written nowadays and opera audiences go to see a relatively small repertory of works again and again; therefore, the only way of introducing variety into the modern, by and large 'fixed' repertory is through different production styles. Furthermore, whereas in the nineteenth century there was a sense that the original staging and visual appearance of the opera was part of the composer's essential conception of the work and integral to the work, ideas about production values have changed. Today we have a rather different concept of artistic freedom and tend to believe that each production should be original – indeed, new productions are sometimes criticized by press reviewers if they are deemed 'safe' or derivative.

A good example of a production in which a producer seems intentionally to have attempted to go against the grain of an inherited performance tradition is that of Verdi's *Aida* created in 2004 by American avant-garde director Robert Wilson for the Théâtre Royal de la Monnaie in Brussels. Visual spectacle is arguably integral to *Aida*: Verdi was attracted to the subject because of its rich scenic detail, and in the Ricordi production book he painstakingly outlined precisely how characters should move in the various processions, ritual crowd scenes and dances. Updated or abstract stagings of *Aida* are something of a rarity: producers have not always followed Verdi's instructions to the letter, but they have usually maintained some degree of visual excess, decking out stages with pyramids and palm trees and sometimes even using live horses or elephants. Wilson, by contrast, swapped lavish scenery for a minimalist play of deep blue lighting and used an unusual, almost motionless style of stage direction influenced by Japanese Noh theatre, in which the singers assume static, stylized poses, consciously avoiding any physical or visual contact with one another. This production was certainly original and arguably dramatically effective in its own way. However, it seemed like a deliberate rejection of any concept of theatricality that would have been recognisable to Verdi, to the extent that we might debate whether an *Aida* without spectacle or movement is actually still Verdi's *Aida*.

Although it might be possible to recreate the original visual aspects of a Verdi opera for which a production book is available, a sceptic might also point to other aspects of the performance that are likely to be far from 'authentic'. For instance, even if the staging manual describes the sorts of gestures a performer ought to make, would a modern singer necessarily interpret these instructions in the same way as a nineteenth-century performer? (Styles of acting in opera were very different in the nineteenth century to those we would expect to see today.) We would also be kidding ourselves if we were to believe ourselves to be getting to the original 'core' of the work simply by staging it in period dress.

If we try to make a performance musically 'authentic' we also run the risk of getting into a potential minefield. Many critical editions of operas have been published in recent years. You might assume that this would make it easy to perform an opera 'authentically', musically speaking. However, these editions cannot provide all of the answers. They cannot tell us what singers from the past actually sounded like (and they undoubtedly sounded different from modern singers) – and we might debate the extent to which it would be desirable for singers today to emulate the mannerisms of past generations.

OPERA IN TRANSLATION

Prior to the twentieth century, audience members would typically purchase the libretto of an opera to read beforehand. These days, if a theatre displays surtitles electronically above the stage we have the opportunity to follow the words as the opera goes along. However, problems arise when a libretto is translated from a foreign language into English. A direct translation of the librettist's words would not necessarily fit the music, and the ends of lines would no longer rhyme. This doesn't particularly matter if you're just reading a libretto or score and understanding the meaning is all that is important; however, it does matter if a translation is being prepared for *performance*, when a foreign-language opera is to be sung in English. In this situation, the translator will have to come up with a translation that maintains the general meaning of the original words and that also fits the flow of the music. So you should take care when following a vocal score that contains what we would call a 'singing translation' – the translation may be only an approximation of the original text, and you shouldn't assume that a given word is a direct translation of the foreign word placed directly above or below it.

It would also be possible to have a prolonged debate about the extent to which modern singers should add vocal ornamentation to operatic arias. As we have seen, in operas from the eighteenth and early nineteenth centuries, singers were expected to embellish the music, so it would seem that singers today ought to do the same in order to be 'authentic', but this leads to further questions. Should modern singers have total liberty to add their own embellishments, or should they examine historical treatises and attempt to imitate the conventions of ornamentation used by singers in the past? Are modern performers even capable of improvising in the way that singers would have been two centuries ago (these skills have arguably been lost)? When a singer is performing the works of a later nineteenth-century composer such as Verdi, the question of ornamentation becomes even more vexed. Verdi's career straddled a period in which the composer's notated score was coming to be regarded as increasingly sacrosanct. Performance practice changed greatly across the course of Verdi's career and indeed may have varied from place to place and from singer to singer.

All of these debates are further complicated by the fact that operas often exist in several different versions, which may date from the composer's own lifetime, if cuts or changes were made for performances in different cities. Throughout opera's history it has been common for small-scale changes to be made to an opera after its first performance or even its first production, as a composer and the rest of the creative team realise that various things do not work. Some operatic revisions, however, have been more large scale. Gluck, for instance, rewrote his opera *Orfeo ed Euridice*, first performed in Vienna in 1762, as *Orphée et Eurydice* when it was performed in Paris in 1774, adapting the work to the tastes of a different audience and the talents and demands of a new cast. The changes Gluck made were fairly substantial: a new French librettist was hired to expand the original text, meaning that Gluck had to write whole new sections of music. The role of Orpheus had to be rewritten as it was now to be performed by an *haute contre* rather than a castrato, in keeping with French taste. Gluck also had to add ballet scenes and adapt the orchestration. A century later, Verdi, as we have already seen, wrote revised versions of several of his operas (including *Macbeth* and *Simon Boccanegra*). In some cases, as with Gluck's *Orfeo ed Euridice*, Verdi was pragmatically adapting a work for a different context; however, in other cases he chose to rewrite an opera simply because he had rethought his conception of how a particular dramatic subject ought to be set as an opera.

These operatic revisions raise a range of intriguing questions. Sometimes the revised version was written several decades after the original opera. Which of these versions should we prioritize? How should we give weight, respectively, to the composer's original conception of a work and to his or her later thoughts? In the case of an opera that a composer has revised on what we might call ideological grounds, we could argue in favour of staging the later version, on the grounds that the composer presumably saw his or her changes as improvements – although perhaps even this would be a simplistic assumption except in instances where a composer has actually withdrawn the original version. In cases where an opera has been revised for more pragmatic reasons, it is more difficult to decide which version to perform today. How can we know which version of his Orpheus opera Gluck preferred, or whether he even had strong feelings about such matters? Should a modern opera company reinstate the ballets that both Gluck and Verdi added to their operas for French theatres but which did not form part of their original conception of the works? Then there is also the question of how to deal with performance conventions that have developed since the composer's death. Sometimes it has become customary to cut passages from certain operas – to what extent should we prioritize this tradition, or should we always go back to the composer's own text?

Moreover, even if we were to attempt to be faithful to the performance styles of earlier centuries, should we attempt to recreate other aspects of the original performance? It would be possible to recreate the exact physical space in which a particular repertory of operas was performed, in a similar way to the establishment in the 1990s of the new Globe Theatre, close to the site of Shakespeare's original on London's South Bank. However, the 'theatrical experience' of a modern audience would be very different to that of earlier audiences. It would be radical indeed to suggest trying to reproduce this, particularly for an opera prior to the mid nineteenth century – audiences behaved very differently back then. In late eighteenth-century London, gentlemen walked from box to box during the performance to pay social calls and went down into the stalls in order to ogle the ladies in the boxes above. Audience members climbed up onto the stage itself when they wanted to take a closer look at the action – and to get a good view of their fellow spectators. Audiences were extremely vocal during the performance, whether demanding encores, hissing, debating politics, gossiping or even rioting. To recreate the authentic experience, one would need to leave the house lights on, redesign the seating and allow audience members to speak and move about throughout the performance.

Few would suggest a return to such conditions, but they were an important part of the theatrical experience at the time. Furthermore, it would be impossible for modern audiences to listen to operas from the nineteenth century (or earlier) with what we might call 'innocent' ears. In other words, we cannot ever hope to recreate the spontaneous response of an audience hearing the opera in question for the very first time, without having heard any of the more recent works that followed (which will inevitably have coloured how modern audiences experience older works). Perhaps it is safest to conclude that we can never recreate operas from the past 'authentically' nor experience them as they were originally experienced. That said, an awareness of historically informed performance practices can certainly be interesting and potentially useful to opera directors.

Updating opera

At the other end of the spectrum, many directors today see updating operas as essential to communicating with a modern audience, helping to get rid of the rather stuffy image with which opera is often perceived to be tainted. Many opera productions today are novel and interesting – sometimes a production draws more attention for its staging and costumes than for its musical aspects and in some cases this even seems to be a deliberate strategy. (I'd point, for example, to a recent production of *Aida* by English National Opera with costumes by fashion designer Zandra Rhodes, which was given a large amount of advance publicity.) Some modern productions are highly successful in striking a chord with contemporary audiences. An example might be the production of *Rigoletto* by theatre director, author and lecturer Jonathan Miller, which has been in the repertory of English National Opera since 1982. *Rigoletto* (an opera I will discuss in more detail in the next chapter) is set in the morally bankrupt court of the sixteenth-century Duke of Mantua, which is part of a wider seedy society, where hired assassins lurk down dark alleyways. Miller transferred the action to mafia-run Little Italy, New York, during the 1950s. The production acknowledges the influence of films such as *The Godfather* as well as the visual influence, in the staging of Act Three, of Edward Hopper's 1942 painting *Nighthawks*. Instead of working as a court jester, Rigoletto works as head waiter in a bar owned by 'Dook', a gang leader.

This production has been very popular and is still regularly revived several decades on. Verdi's central concerns – outer ugliness vs inner beauty, the underworld, rape – map equally well on to a twentieth-century setting. This production is generally agreed to have genuinely updated the opera in a vital and popular way, whilst remaining entirely faithful to Verdi's original message. The twentieth-century setting made the psychological situation particularly vivid to a modern audience and pointed out the universality of Verdi's themes, without Miller having tried to impose some sort of external, political message upon the work. Miller said of this production: 'Here the social world of the original court mapped completely, without any of the points having to be dislocated, onto the social world of the mafia.' On the other hand, some more radical directors might be critical of a production such as this, arguing that Miller had merely engaged in a spot of picturesque but conservative window-dressing, not reinterpreting the meaning of the work for modern audiences in any significant way.

Some modern productions have been much more controversial than those discussed so far. Often today, a director puts together a 'concept' production and sometimes such concepts are explicitly political or deliberately intended to shock. Many opera houses have had to issue advance warnings to let potential audience members know that a particular production involves nudity, but this may be less shocking than the events that are acted out on stage. In a recent production of *Rigoletto* at the Royal Opera House by David McVicar, the party scene was reminiscent of an orgy, making Miller's production look tame indeed. But other directors have gone further still in adding a sexual element to their productions. A particularly controversial opera director is Spanish theatre director Calixto Bieito, who has worked extensively for opera companies across Europe. His production of Verdi's *Un ballo in maschera* (*A Masked Ball*, 1859), first staged at the Gran Teatre del Liceu in Barcelona in 2001, caused a scandal, for incorporating a scene in the gents' toilet at the parliament and a male rape scene, both of which were completely extraneous to anything in Verdi's original version. When the production transferred to London (English National Opera), the tenor lead took the unusual decision of dropping out on the grounds that he wanted his children to be able to come and see him in the opera.

Bieito's production of Mozart's *Die Entführung aus dem Serail* ('The Abduction from the Harem', 1782) at the Komische Oper in Berlin was similarly gratuitous, transposing the action to a desolate, violent and at times gruesome underworld of sex and drugs, a setting that would have been completely alien to Mozart and his librettist. If sexually explicit scenes have become par for the course in some modern opera productions, so too have scenes of drug taking. For instance, American director Peter Sellars has updated Mozart to modern New York, depicting Don Giovanni peddling heroin in the Bronx. Sellars uses drug addiction as an explanation of why the character Donna Anna is so attached to Don Giovanni – clearly this goes way beyond anything the opera's original creators would have envisaged.

Productions like these often prompt a great deal of controversy and heated reactions from the press. Looking beyond gut reactions, however, what are the pros and cons of such productions? Do they make operas more relevant to modern life or do they take liberties, creating scandal for scandal's sake, tampering with revered works of art in the process? We might argue that updated productions are problematic when they are so extreme that they detract from the action unfolding on stage – either with incongruous costumes or sets or when the stage business seems to obtrude excessively into the drama or is gratuitous for its own sake – or when they distort the narrative with a message projected by the director. Some productions have been highly political in intent, drawing explicit correlations with contemporary political or social situations, creating an opera far removed from what the composer originally intended. This has led to the view in some quarters that directors today are given too much power; the expression 'producer's opera' or 'director's opera' has become a pejorative one.

On the other hand, we might question the extent to which the composer's original intentions (even if we can gain access to them) *ought* to be revered today. There have been debates in all Humanities subjects in recent years about 'the death of the author', an idea coined in the late 1960s by the French literary critic Roland Barthes. Put simply, Barthes sees an art-work and its author as distinct from one another and encourages critics to liberate themselves from taking the author's intentions into account when interpreting a work of art. This idea has very much been behind the rise of reception studies in all branches of the Humanities, in which the responses of readers (in the case of literary works), audiences (in the case of drama or music) and critics become as interesting a focus of study as the creator of the artwork him or herself. If we apply this idea to opera production, we might say that the director has the right to reinterpret the opera's action in any way he or she sees fit. Some directors and critics today might see the composer's original message or conception of their work as almost entirely irrelevant – reinterpretation is everything. And in fact, the idea of a composer and librettist being the sole creators, indeed the 'owners' of an opera, is very much a nineteenth-century one. In earlier centuries it was far more normal to see an opera as the product of a large number of different creative agents.

However, we might argue that some opera directors have created particularly shocking productions in recent years simply to create a sense of notoriety and to draw attention to themselves – a cynic might say that vanity and possibly even financial gain are the motivations behind their productions. The directors in turn would be likely to argue back, saying that their intention has been to shake opera audiences out of their comfort zone. It is worth remembering that operas have always been political in various ways and have often created controversy – these issues will be discussed further in the next chapter. Some directors would probably argue that the issues that shocked and challenged audiences in previous centuries do not always have the same impact upon us today, and that their productions merely substitute new issues that are designed to make audiences think and question their prejudices. Perhaps modern productions ought to be unsettling, forcing us to challenge our musical and dramatic assumptions about a work.

We could argue that it is important to approach old operatic favourites in new ways – that they only remain meaningful if we allow their meanings to shift with time. New productions can offer new 'readings' of a familiar work, encouraging us to rethink our understanding of a particular opera. It is possible to imagine extreme scenarios, whereby, on the one hand, directors strive for historical 'authenticity' to such an extent that operas became stale 'museum pieces', and, on the other, directors take liberties with operas that extend as far as recomposing the music or changing the text. In the middle, however, there are myriad different ways of presenting opera, ranging from traditional, lavish, neo-Romantic stagings to pared-down stagings in modern dress. Whatever we may think of the 'extremes' of opera production, the diversity of operatic stagings today and the fact that opera attracts experimental directors and designers shows that it is still a vibrant, exciting art-form.

Operatic spaces old and new

In recent years our assumptions about operatic performance – and about the audience for opera – have been challenged by the fact that operas are increasingly being performed in a variety of places and spaces outside the traditional opera house. Some of the clichés about opera as an inaccessible art-form stem from the physical spaces in which operas have traditionally been performed. You might think that the building in which an opera is performed is irrelevant to an audience's experience of the operatic performance itself, yet the architecture and interior décor of a public building may be read as being inscribed with social meaning and ideological values. Older opera houses send out a message about their place in society at the time when they were built: they tend to be grand, highly decorative buildings that resemble palaces or appear to have been modelled upon Grecian temples. These references invoke power and prestige and also suggest that opera houses are literally 'temples' of art, shrines where the audience come to worship in awe-struck silence, perhaps, rather than welcoming places of entertainment.

In the style of auditorium typical of many older opera houses, the seating arrangement is an overt physical representation of a hierarchical class structure: the most expensive seats, with the best views, are roughly on a level with the stage, with the seats becoming cheaper and less comfortable as one ascends to the gallery or 'gods'. Most eighteenth- and nineteenth-century opera houses were horseshoe shaped with privately owned boxes arranged in tiers, and took their cue from the earliest Italian opera houses of the seventeenth century, which in turn were modelled upon the amphitheatres of ancient Greece and Rome. However, some theatres, such as the Royal Opera House in London, opened up many of their boxes during the nineteenth century, when long-standing family subscriptions expired, in order to create a more democratic audience space, perhaps leaving just a few boxes near to the stage for VIPs or for ceremonial purposes.

Today the overt displays of power presented by many traditional opera houses can prompt mixed emotions. Going to such an opera house is like stepping back in time to a gilded age. Some audience members will identify with this architecture and with the values it seems to represent. For others it may seem intimidating or off-putting, reinforcing everything they ever suspected about opera being for the wealthy and suggesting that only those who enjoy a particular degree of social prestige are welcome inside such buildings. A third group may simply find such buildings historically interesting or see the elaborate architecture of nineteenth-century opera houses as part of the conscious spectacle of opera, a counterpart to the elaborate sets and clever stage machinery that have dazzled opera audiences for centuries. But whether opera houses inspire identification, aspiration or alienation, there seems to be no getting away from the fact that this architecture tells a story about a privileged past.

On the other hand, one might argue that nineteenth-century opera houses do not look so dissimilar from other civic buildings of their day: in Britain they are scarcely different in their appearance to contemporary town halls (the town hall in Birmingham city centre, for instance, was modelled upon the Parthenon), or even banks that can still be found on many high streets. So perhaps this style of architecture was not intended to signal exclusivity so much as a sense of civic pride, in which the whole community could share. Opera houses were grand buildings because they were important civic meeting places and because opera itself was recognized to be an important medium through which society debated the most vital issues of the day.

Today it would be inconceivable to build this sort of opera house. Opera house design has changed radically in the twentieth century for a number of reasons. Firstly, architects now have to work within greater economic constraints, reflecting a decline in aristocratic patronage and arguably opera's waning place in society. Furthermore, most architects naturally desire to appear cutting-edge and are reluctant to design buildings that smack of pastiche. However, there is undoubtedly another agenda at stake: many architects of modern opera houses have either consciously striven or been instructed to be more 'democratic' in their designs, so that their buildings send out a different message to the opera houses of old.

AN ICONIC NINETEENTH-CENTURY OPERA HOUSE

The Paris Opéra, first opened to the public in 1875, has another name, the 'Palais Garnier', after its architect, Charles Garnier. That use of the word 'palace' is striking: even the Republican French drew upon the rhetoric of royalty in constructing their public buildings during the nineteenth century. Garnier aimed for splendour and luxury throughout his building, both within and without. The theatre was part of a grand civic vision: it occupies a dramatic position in central Paris, standing at the intersection of several of Baron Haussmann's grand new boulevards, with the Avénue de l'Opéra affording the visitor a splendid approach to the opera house. Externally the building is characterized by columns and quasi-Grecian statues representing the music of a selection of canonical composers. Step inside and the trappings of power and luxury continue: here we find chandeliers, highly ornate marble carvings and yet more classical columns. And at the heart of it all is an extravagantly grand, over-sized staircase, designed to accommodate the sweep of hundreds of long-trained gowns. This staircase itself was designed to become a part of the performative experience: Garnier constructed balconies (akin to those inside the auditorium itself) overlooking the staircase, from which audience members could watch others make their grand entrance.

In commissioning the Opéra de la Bastille (Paris's newer opera house, opened in 1990), President François Mitterrand was trying to regenerate a formerly somewhat run-down area of Paris and to create an institution that would provide 'opera for all'. With these aims in mind, it would arguably have been inappropriate to use a style of architecture redolent of the 'old' operatic values: the new opera house is a curved building clad in glass and stone. A similar spirit of regeneration underpinned the construction in New York of the new Metropolitan Opera House (1966) as part of the Lincoln Center, a complex of concert halls and performance spaces in what had been a run-down part of the Upper West Side. (Appropriately, the opera house opened with a new opera by an American composer – *Antony and Cleopatra* by Samuel Barber – signalling the opera house's symbolic commitment to the future.) The Sydney Opera House (1973), meanwhile, is so striking that it has become a symbol of the city in a way that seems to signal that opera is for all and make a statement about Australia's status as a 'new' nation.

Nowadays a brief for the interior of a new opera house will place a high emphasis upon physical accessibility and upon making core areas of the theatre 'open access', allowing a wide range of people to take part in the activities of the theatre even if they are not watching a production in the main auditorium. (These might range from simply having a drink in the opera house cafeteria to visiting an exhibition of costumes or hearing a recital by young artists affiliated to the opera house.) Furthermore, many operas are now performed outside the opera house altogether. As part of their outreach programmes, opera companies are increasingly taking opera to new and unexpected places – going out to find new audiences in the hope that these audiences will ultimately come to them. Outreach projects include pre-performance talks open to all, schools' projects and activities for families, and community projects working with prisoners or underprivileged social groups. We could point to numerous examples of operas being staged in unexpected places.

Recently, for instance, there has been a trend for presenting operas in public places such as railway stations. In 2004 the British Broadcasting Corporation (BBC) put on a specially created opera (*Flashmob the Opera*) during the rush hour at London's Paddington Station, also broadcasting the performance on BBC Three, a television station aimed at viewers aged between fifteen and thirty-four. The new opera engaged with everyday preoccupations and interests (it featured a love triangle and a man's passion for football), and used well-known music from operas by Mozart, Rossini, Bizet, Verdi and Puccini that would probably be familiar even to listeners who considered themselves to know little about opera. The resources used included four soloists, the BBC Concert Orchestra and several separate choruses, including one of football supporters and singers from the BBC. A video of the performance was projected onto screens so that passengers throughout the station could follow the action. The singers moved around as the opera unfolded, to locations including the concourse, a sushi bar and pub, and onto the platforms themselves: the station, meanwhile, remained operational throughout the event. To those passing through, this must have seemed an intriguing spectacle. It was designed to whet the curiosity of both passing commuters and a young audience at home who might not previously have encountered opera and who might have preconceived ideas about it. By relocating opera to an 'everyday' setting, the organizers showed that it is something that engages with topics that affect all of us, and from the comments BBC Three viewers left on internet message boards it would seem that the experiment generated a positive response.

Similarly, in 2008 commuters at Zurich station and television viewers in Switzerland had the opportunity to watch a special performance of Verdi's *La traviata*. Again, the opera was presented 'on the move' with scenes enacted in the station's main hall, on platforms and in a coffee shop. The nature of this project was slightly different, of course: the singers were performing an established opera rather than a newly devised work. One might argue, on the one hand, that this was more conservative, or on the other that it was more daring, in presenting potentially new audiences with the 'real thing' rather than what a cynic might call 'opera-lite', written expressly to appeal to an audience unfamiliar with opera.

Both of these experiments presented practical, logistical and acoustical challenges for the performers and broadcasters. Moreover, they raised interesting and potentially problematic questions about the way in which we conventionally watch opera and alternative ways in which we might. Commuters passing through a railway station would be unlikely to stay to watch the opera in its entirety, even if the viewers of the British and Swiss television stations might. Yet operas contain a developing musical and dramatic narrative: you can't really 'drop in' for part of it. Or can you? Operas have always been considered 'fragmentable' in various ways. For instance, favourite operatic tunes were performed independently in concert by nineteenth-century *prima donnas* in just the same way as they feature on 'opera's greatest hits'-type albums today. And back in the eighteenth and early nineteenth centuries, audiences at the opera house did not typically devote their rapt attention to the performance on stage – as explained earlier, the occupants of the boxes would also be engaged in socializing, eating, gambling and so forth during the performance and would often only concentrate during the 'best bits'. Later in the nineteenth century, opera came to be regarded less as entertainment and more as art, the house lights were lowered and audiences were expected to pay attention and listen in silence – any noise in the opera house today is likely to be greeted by outraged tutting from fellow audience members. But perhaps this new approach to opera, in which one can 'drop in and out', is merely a return to an older model of opera as entertainment.

Of course, the most democratic ways of disseminating opera have come through technology. Operatic highlights featured prominently in record companies' catalogues from the earliest days of recording technology (in 1904 opera singer Enrico Caruso became the first artist to sell a million records). In subsequent decades, of course, it became possible for people to experience entire operas in the comfort of their own homes, through long-play records (later CDs), videos and DVDs. However, some people still yearn to experience opera in a communal setting and the technology of film has made this possible for those who are unable to attend a live performance. A particularly interesting recent development has been the regular live relays of operas from the Metropolitan Opera in New York that audiences can watch in cinemas all over North America and Europe. But opera and film have been intimately linked since the beginning of the twentieth century. The next section explores recent debates that have taken place regarding the intersection of these two genres and whether filmed opera may even constitute a whole new art-form in its own right.

Opera on film

Directors have been drawn to opera from the very earliest days of film. The number of films of operas or based on opera-related themes is demonstrated by the sheer weight and physical size of Ken Wlaschin's recent *Encyclopedia of Opera on Screen*, which runs to over 850 pages. There was a particular vogue for films based on operas between 1908 and 1910. There were numerous reasons why opera should have offered an attraction to early film directors. Firstly, opera was arguably one of the most important forms of entertainment of its day (it is somewhat ironic that cinema would, of course, jeopardize that popularity). Thus it seemed logical to transfer the most popular stories with which opera audiences were familiar to the new medium of film, since they would have, in effect, a ready-made audience. For instance, many early films were adaptations of Gounod's *Faust* (1859), an opera that had been phenomenally popular in European and American opera houses in the late nineteenth century, and which had the added bonus of featuring magical scenes which allowed directors to show off film's potential for visual trickery.

FILM DIRECTORS AT THE OPERA

Many renowned film directors have been tempted to try their hand at the medium of opera, whether directing stage productions or creating opera films. One of the most famous is Italian director Franco Zeffirelli who has created productions for theatres in Europe and the USA since the 1950s, many of which have come to be seen as iconic in their own right. For instance, his lavish, traditional 1964 production of *Tosca* for the Royal Opera House in London, originally created for a cast including Maria Callas and Tito Gobbi, was used by the theatre for forty years and mounted 240 times. Celebrated film directors who have created productions for opera houses in recent years include Woody Allen, who directed Puccini's *Gianni Schicchi* (1918) for the Los Angeles Opera in 2008. Directors who have transferred operas to film have often been able to be more experimental in their approach than those working for opera houses. Whereas some have exploited the added realism that film allows, Swedish film director Ingmar Bergman intercut shots of the audience and the stage action in his 1975 film of *The Magic Flute*, even showing backstage shots and changing scenery, as if to offer a commentary on the self-conscious theatricality of opera.

In recent years, musicologists have started to take an interest in 'screen opera'. Scholars of opera on film have certainly developed new and interesting ways of interpreting this genre, often drawing fruitfully upon theories developed in the study of film since the 1950s. Marcia Citron has posited early cinema as a logical successor to opera and suggests that the two media had much in common – both were 'hyper-dramatic' forms of entertainment – and that early cinema learnt much, in particular, from the gestures and dramatic excesses of the then highly popular *Verismo* opera. (In turn, there has been a two-way exchange of influence: opera composers themselves had much to learn from the world of early film. Puccini, for example, is often cited as a composer whose operas work in a quasi-filmic manner.) However, early opera films differed in one crucial respect from the operas people saw at the theatre – they were silent! It may seem rather strange that the directors of silent movies were drawn to opera at all. However, silent films weren't really silent, of course: an accompanying 'soundtrack' would have been provided either by a phonograph record or in the form of an arrangement played by the cinema pianist – singers might even perform live in the cinema. However, the musical accompaniment given to a single 'silent' opera film would have varied from cinema to cinema, beyond any form of centralized directorial control.

Today, of course, opera films have soundtracks and, musically speaking, can be similar to a production in a theatre. However, there are many respects in which films of operas differ from operas as performed on the stage. One of the most obvious practical differences is that films can use exterior locations. Whereas a theatre has to 'mock up' an illusion of an opera's setting – whether this be the Scottish Highlands, the pyramids at Giza or a Venetian canal – cast and crew can actually go to the location in question when making an opera film. This creates the capacity to depict vast panoramas, something that can be highly impressive. Furthermore, the capacity for opera films to be shot on location arguably adds to a sense of 'realism' – something audiences throughout the twentieth century increasingly came to expect from entertainment, whether in the form of film or television.

However, this raises potential questions or problems and may not be entirely welcome. The settings may look realistic, but singing as a means of communication is never going to be realistic, and thus the two may seem bizarrely at odds. Some viewers may lament the loss of the consciously 'theatrical' aspects of opera, for example, the element of 'illusion' that has the capacity to leave us spellbound – when it is taken out of the opera house for which it, as an art-form, was conceived. Outdoor performances present practical challenges that may further reduce the 'theatrical' element. It is difficult for performers to record operas on location – although it has been done in some films – because of acoustical challenges and the question of where the orchestra should be placed. Thus, singers (or even actors) sometimes lip-synch to a pre-recorded 'soundtrack', a practice that can not only look artificial and unconvincing, but which removes the thrill one gets in the opera house (and which is captured to some degree in videos of stage productions) of watching and listening to a singer performing almost heroic feats of musical virtuosity live. In other words, an element of the distinctive 'magic' of opera is arguably lost, as, of course, is the audience's live response, and their capacity to shape the operatic experience.

Another obvious respect in which a filmed opera differs from an opera on stage is that the camera acts as a sort of intermediary between audience and performers. The camera has the potential to do close ups – to focus in on particular characters as they sing and react to the drama. This, of course, brings a wonderful element of expressiveness to the performance, drawing the audience into the action in a way that is not possible in the opera house, where most audience members apart from those in the expensive seats are seated too far away from the stage to be able to see the performers' faces. On the other hand, of course, elements of the theatrical experience are compromised: if a camera chooses to focus upon a particular character, the audience is deprived of the 'bigger picture' that they would see in the opera house: in other words, it is the director who chooses what we focus upon rather than us. Thus, the camera becomes an extremely powerful agent in shaping the audience's experience.

This is an issue that has long concerned theorists. Walter Benjamin addressed it in his 1936 essay 'The Work of Art in the Age of Mechanical Reproduction' (originally published in a

German journal called *Zeitschrift für Sozialforschung*). Benjamin's central thesis is that each work of art is embedded in a unique context and that in reproducing a work of art multiple times we strip it of its distinctive 'aura'. He writes about the difference between an actor performing on stage and for the camera, lamenting the fact that the camera does not respect the performance as an integral whole, with the result that the cameraman (or, at one remove, the director) becomes the 'author' of the performance rather than the performer him or herself. More recently, Marcia Citron, referring specifically to Franco Zeffirelli's film of *La traviata*, has admitted that she feels uncomfortable about some directors' tendency to manipulate our emotions through huge close ups in ways that feel, to her, exploitative. Thus, the camera intervenes in the operatic experience, telling us where to look and how to feel.

This chapter has aimed to illustrate a few of the critical approaches that have been taken by scholars to the performance and production of opera in recent years. These are by no means the only issues that have preoccupied them. Another expanding area within opera studies focuses upon singers. Some scholars have taken a biographical approach, investigating singers' careers and examining the role individual singers played in shaping (co-authoring even) individual operas. Others have drawn upon psychoanalytical theories of the 'voice' or have scrutinized responses to particular singers, either by individuals or by society at large. Particular attention has been paid to arguably the most alluring and celebrated of operatic performers, the *prima donna* (although scholars are increasingly taking an interest in male singers from the past – the divo, if you like, as well as the diva). So, the field of what we might loosely refer to as 'production studies' is wide and diverse. Let's turn now to an equally lively area of contemporary debate – how operas have engaged in a variety of fascinating ways with politics.

3

Opera and politics

Opera can be 'political' in a variety of ways. Usually, when we refer to opera and politics, we are not talking about politics in the party political sense. Rather, operas may be considered political because their libretti treat subjects that were considered to be politically contentious at the time they were first written: these may include nationalism, empire, monarchy, social hierarchies or gender politics. Some composers have deliberately set out to convey political messages in their works. Other, less politically engaged composers may have had no such intention, yet their works may have acquired political resonance nevertheless. Operas sometimes become politicized through criticism and reception, as audiences and critics read political messages and social significance into operas that may go beyond the composer and librettist's original intentions. Both 'political' and 'politicized' operas will be discussed in this chapter. However, there are yet more ways in which an opera may become political. Some stagings of operas are governed by political motivations, as we have already seen in Chapter Two: an updating of a nineteenth-century opera that shifts the staging to the recent Iraq war, for instance, would give the opera political resonance that would speak particularly vividly to a new audience. And finally, another way of talking about opera and politics would be to debate the political implications of opera as an institution through the ages and in different cultures.

Opera and politics have been intertwined since the very earliest days of the art-form. Originally, as you will recall from Chapter One, operas were typically written with the primary aim of glorifying wealthy patrons. The composers and librettists who wrote the earliest court operas were effectively servants, but many later artists were also often happy to uphold the political status quo through their works. French operas by composers such as Lully and Rameau were a conscious display of prestige and political power; the Italian *opera seria* genre of the eighteenth century mythologized kings and other rulers as heroes and forces for good, and encouraged audiences to venerate them. However, later composers and librettists increasingly used their works to challenge existing power structures. Thus, opera can be political either in the sense of speaking for or against a political regime. It is true that there are many operas about people in positions of power or privilege, something that may lead to accusations of opera being about upper-class concerns. However, the stories that many later operas tell are about ordinary people overthrowing figures of authority and operas have often engaged in criticising rather than supporting social elites.

A particularly well-known example of an opera that treats the subject of class conflict is Mozart's *The Marriage of Figaro* (*Le nozze di Figaro*), set to a libretto by Lorenzo Da Ponte and first performed in Vienna in 1786. The opera is a story of sexual and class power relations in which ordinary people get the better of their masters, and in which the vulnerability and humanity of everyone involved is celebrated. A clever servant, Figaro, and his fellow servants manage to outwit their employer, the Count Almaviva. The Count wishes to seduce Figaro's fiancée, Susanna, but the servants expose his game and he is forced to beg his wife the Countess for forgiveness. The household therefore challenges the 'droit du seigneur' – the practice whereby a nobleman had the right to sleep with any female servant in his employ on her wedding night, before her husband – and, moreover, leaves him looking rather stupid.

This subject was politically contentious from the start: it was based on a play by the French playwright Pierre-Augustin Beaumarchais, first performed in Paris in 1784 after having been banned in Vienna. In order to understand why the plot – which may seem fairly innocuous to us – was deemed so controversial and offensive, we need to remember the social and political tensions of the period in which the play and the opera were staged. Both were written and performed in the lead-up to the French Revolution of 1789, when social tensions were rife, and at a time when the principles of Enlightenment philosophy were leading many to question the idea of absolute monarchy. The growing unrest in Paris was deeply troubling to members of the Austrian (Habsburg) monarchy, who feared similar develop-ments might take place at home. Indeed, the growing hostility towards the monarchy in France felt very close to home indeed to the Habsburgs in Vienna, despite their geographical distance. This was because the royal families of Europe were closely inter-connected: Queen Marie Antoinette of France, who would, within a few years, become one of the most famous victims of the guillotine, was the sister of Emperor Joseph II of Austria and had been born and bred in Vienna. One assumes that Mozart and Da Ponte had some sympathy with the anti-aristocratic subject matter of Beaumarchais's play (Da Ponte in particular is known to have held radical political views), although the opera's tone could reasonably be said to be somewhat less revolutionary than the play.

The difficulties Beaumarchais encountered in getting his play staged – and Mozart and Da Ponte's efforts to be more cautious – remind us, however, that artists, including composers and librettists, certainly did not have an entirely free rein, even after traditional court patronage began to loosen its grip. Those in power realized relatively early on in opera's history that the art-form had the capacity to be politically contentious. Thus, in many societies operas were subject to scrutiny by the censors, although the degree of censorship a composer might face varied from country to country (even from city to city, in the case of the Italian peninsula), and from period to period. Composers

WOLFGANG AMADEUS MOZART

Born in Salzburg in 1756, Wolfgang Amadeus Mozart was a child prodigy who began composing at the age of five. He mastered all the major musical genres of his day – the symphony, the concerto, chamber music, choral music and opera – and wrote a prolific number of works during his short life. (He would die in 1791 at the age of just thirty-five.) Mozart lived at a time when patterns of patronage for musicians were changing. Whereas his slightly older contemporary Joseph Haydn experienced a traditional patronage arrangement, working for many years at the Esterhaza court, Mozart was not able to find an aristocratic patron and had to try and patch together a living from teaching, publishing and from performances of his music. Although in some senses liberating, this made for a precarious lifestyle, and Mozart is believed to have died a pauper. He wrote in all of the main operatic genres of his day – *opera seria*, *opera buffa* and the new German genre of the *Singspiel*. His works are generally felt to have stood the test of time not only because of their beautiful music, but because they transcended the dramatic conventions of the day with their psychological credibility.

and librettists therefore found ways of critiquing power structures that were subtle enough to escape the censor's gaze but powerful enough to ensure that their essential message was still conveyed effectively to the audience. As a case study, let's turn now to a composer who suffered particular problems with the censor and who is often held up as one of the most politically active of opera composers: Giuseppe Verdi.

Verdi and nationalism

In nineteenth-century Italy, opera and politics were intimately linked. Opera was an extremely popular form of entertainment:

every town had its opera house and people would attend the same production time and time again. But the opera house was also an important civic meeting place, where people discussed politics and conducted business meetings. These discussions did not only take place in the foyers of opera houses: operas themselves were often used as vehicles through which political messages might be disseminated.

Few composers have been as actively involved in politics as Verdi. He took part in the important political debates of his day, even becoming a deputy in the Turin parliament and representing his local area during the early 1860s. (However, we should note that Verdi wasn't allied with a particular party as such, and his views on politics as expressed privately were varied and contradictory.) Even in old age he was involved in politics through charitable acts, founding, building and managing a small hospital near his estate in Parma, and a large retirement home for musicians in Milan, which is still operating today.

As a younger man, in the 1840s and 1850s, Verdi was involved in the drive towards Italian unification, and this was a theme that he and his librettists alluded to on several occasions in his operas. Before turning to think about these works, it's important to know a bit about the political context of early nineteenth-century Italy. Certain clichéd associations probably spring to mind when we think of Italy – piazzas, pizza and ice cream, perhaps; Renaissance palazzi or ancient Roman remains – so it can be surprising to learn that Italy as a national identity didn't actually exist until relatively recent history. Prior to the mid nineteenth century, the Italian peninsula was divided into lots of separate states, ruled by individual kings, princes, dukes or the Pope (with the exception of Venice, which was a Republic, as we have seen). By Verdi's time, many parts of what we now call Italy had been under foreign rule for centuries. The north and north east, centring on Milan and Venice, were dominated by Austria; the House of Savoy controlled the Piedmont area around Turin (known as the Kingdom of Sardinia); the Pope controlled Rome and the surrounding area; whilst a Spanish branch of the Bourbon dynasty controlled the south (an area then known as the Kingdom of the Two Sicilies). Italy had not, in fact, been a united nation since Roman times and for this reason there were different regional traditions and dialects – many people did not speak what we might call the standard Italian language. Thus, there was virtually no sense of what it meant to be Italian.

However, a movement began to develop in the early nineteenth century calling for the unification of the Italian states and the expulsion of the foreign occupiers. This movement was called the 'Risorgimento', which means 'to rise again', and by the 1820s various surges of dissent were beginning to manifest themselves through revolutions in cities up and down the peninsula. A revolutionary called Giuseppe Mazzini led the way in calling for a united Italy free of foreign rule, and tried to spark uprisings through the publication of a journal called *La Giovine Italia*, which was widely banned. Over the years that followed, various uprisings, revolutions and battles took place until most of Italy (except Venice and Rome) was unified by 1860. The process was completed by 1871, when the capital of the new nation moved from Turin (via Florence) to Rome.

The arts had an important role to play in the drive towards unification. Risorgimento activists sought to encourage a sense of shared 'Italianness' and literature, art and music could be employed as useful tools in this process. Opera was particularly useful because it was extremely popular and was understood even by the many Italians (especially in the south) who were illiterate and therefore incapable of reading political literature. The opera house also became a place of protest. At performances in Austrian-ruled Venice, for example, audiences threw red, white and green bouquets onto the stage. While this might sound harmless enough, it was in fact highly symbolic, for these were the colours that had been chosen to represent the new Italy. The authorities understood the symbolism and banned such gestures.

Verdi's operas straddled the period of Italian unification and he incorporated a variety of political themes into his works. An example of a consciously patriotic work was his early opera *La battaglia di Legnano*, which Verdi was inspired to write by the political uprisings of 1848. It told the story of Barbarossa's defeat at the hands of the Lombard League at Legnano in 1176 and promoted a vision of a united Italy. Another consciously political opera was *I Lombardi alla prima crociata* ('The Lombards on the First Crusade'). The Milanese audience at the premiere in 1843 is reputed to have identified with the crusading Lombards and to have seen the Saracens controlling the Holy Land as a metaphor for the Austrian rulers who controlled their own city. Other early Verdi operas – whether set in an Italian context or not – were filled with conspiracy plots, appeals for freedom, protests against tyrannical rulers and debate about the effect of government upon people's lives, all of which would have been understood by audiences as politically inflammatory. Verdi was often forced to make his point through allegory, rather than depicting current events on stage, because as we shall see shortly, censorship of opera at this time was strict.

Verdi's works were successful in rallying the people of the Italian states around the cause of unification. This was achieved in particular through his use of opera choruses. As the Risorgimento gained momentum in the 1830s and 1840s, the philosopher and patriot Mazzini called for a more significant role to be accorded to the operatic chorus, to match the egalitarian spirit of the age. Around this time the Italian opera chorus began to move from serving a purely decorative, 'scene-setting' function to participating more fully in the action and dominating long stretches of a work. Operatic choruses could be used to represent 'the voice of the people', which was very fitting for a new age of democracy. It's important to realize, however, that choruses had been employed in this way in France for some time and that Verdi was strongly influenced by the French Grand Operas that used large-scale choruses to represent societies in conflict.

In his more political operas, Verdi built up the drama not so much around a small group of individuals (as he would do in many of his later works) but around a conflict on an international scale. In Verdi's early operas, some choruses played a directly political role, representing struggling nations or political groups. For example, the opera *Ernani* features a chorus of rebels who are plotting against the King of Spain. Even a setting of a Shakespeare play gained contemporary political resonance: *Macbeth* might seem to be an unlikely choice of opera through which to express a desire for Italian unification, but Verdi inserted a chorus of Scottish exiles who sing about their 'oppressed fatherland'. The symbolism was obvious.

But one opera chorus in particular has been considered to be an especially important symbol of Verdi's political ideals. *Nabucco*, first performed in 1842, was the opera that established Verdi's reputation as a national figure: it was such a success that impresarios all over Italy became keen to engage this talented young composer. *Nabucco* tells a story from the Old Testament about the invasion of Jerusalem by the Babylonians (led by King Nebuchadnezzar – Italianized as 'Nabucco') and the capture of the Israelites. The parallels between the opera's subject matter and Italy's situation in the 1840s are easy to discern: the opera was about a chosen nation dreaming of freedom from foreign bondage and the Hebrew slaves were clearly intended to represent the Italians, struggling against their Austrian oppressors. In a particularly symbolic moment, the enslaved Israelites sit by the river Euphrates and sigh for their lost homeland in a chorus entitled 'Va pensiero sull'ali dorate' ('Fly, thought, on wings of gold'). This chorus is not only the most famous number in

Nabucco but one of best-known pieces of music composed by Verdi. It was deliberately simple and set primarily in unison, which made it all the more effective. Verdi's use of unison voices was a compelling way of representing both the solidarity of the Hebrew slaves and – metaphorically – the struggle of the Italians. In an era when Italy was still divided and unification was several decades away, to hear 'the nation' singing as one had powerful political resonance. Moreover, this particular chorus was simple and memorable enough to be sung or hummed by untrained singers. It has gone down in the history books as fact that the chorus was almost immediately taken up as a sort of hymn for Italian unification and that people went around singing it spontaneously outside of the opera house.

It's an appealing story. However, the situation was rather more complicated in reality. Recent scholarship has cast doubt upon the credibility of the claim that Verdi was immediately proclaimed by the Italian people as the bard of Italian nationalism through spontaneous demonstrations and appropriations of his music. Roger Parker (in *Arpa d'or dei fatidici vati*) and Mary-Ann Smart (in her essay 'Verdi, Italian Romanticism, and the Risorgimento') have argued that the facts surrounding the premiere of *Nabucco* were distorted by Verdi's biographers in the later nineteenth and early twentieth centuries, in order to mythologize the composer. In fact, they claim, there is not very much evidence in the documentary sources from the time of *Nabucco* to support the legend. They argue that authors have created evidence where it did not exist, citing Verdi's biographers Monaldi (1878), Soffredini (1910), Gatti (1931) and Abbiati (1959) as having created an ever more embellished version of events. Abbiati's 1959 biography quotes a review of the *Nabucco* premiere at La Scala in 1842 reporting that the audience demanded an encore despite an Austrian ban on repetitions. This story has been repeated by later biographers of Verdi, and it has even been claimed that this event led to encores being demanded at other theatres, with the whole audience joining in. But in fact, Parker and Smart have argued, the quotation Abbiati cites does not appear in the original review that he mentions.

Parker explains that it is difficult to find evidence of the chorus having been taken up as a nationalist hymn in the way that some biographers have suggested, and writes that 'the business of falsifying reviews for early performances of *Nabucco* seems to have been something of a habit among Italian biographers'. Furthermore, other aspects of the 'Va pensiero' legend are to be mistrusted. It has often been said that as Verdi's coffin was transported through the streets of Milan in 1901, the crowd of some 30,000 onlookers spontaneously burst into singing the famous *Nabucco* chorus. Once again, however, the facts have been embellished. The crowd did indeed sing the chorus, but the event was staged: they were conducted by Toscanini rather than bursting into spontaneous song.

Thus, while Verdi was certainly involved in politics and his works have come to accrue political resonance for Italians, it is important not to over-state the case. There was clearly a link between Verdi's operas and the political mood of the day but Parker and Smart caution that we should avoid drawing simple connections between art and society without really researching the facts. However, even if the story about 'Va pensiero' never actually happened, the fact that the story was invented later and embellished by successive biographers is still interesting in its own right, because it is a very clear example of how a composer can become mythologized and 'politicized' through later writings.

Verdi undoubtedly came to be regarded as an extremely important political figure as his career went on and was held up as a political hero during his own lifetime. By the 1850s, Verdi's name was often spelled out as an acronym – the letters V.E.R.D.I. were used to represent the words 'Vittorio Emanuele, Re d'Italia', 'Victor Emanuel, King of Italy'. (Victor

Emanuel was the King of Piedmont, Savoy and Sardinia, who would go on to become the first King of Italy in 1861: many Italian cities have monuments or arcades named in his honour.) Thus, shouting 'Viva Verdi' or daubing the slogan on a wall was a way of being subversive.

Verdi's battle with the censor

Many of Verdi's later operas seem at first sight to be less overtly concerned with politics (in the case of operas from after 1860 this is unsurprising – after 1861 the issue of political unification was no longer relevant). From the 1850s onwards, Verdi became increasingly interested in exploring the psychology of individuals who are placed in difficult personal circumstances. However, one might still read these works as having a certain degree of political resonance. Indeed, they were read by people at the time as such, as can be seen by the intervention of the censor. The censors were extremely powerful in nineteenth-century Italy. They were aware that composers used their operas to portray political intrigue, and that their works often had the potential to be politically inflammatory. The censors were also aware that opera houses, as places where large groups of people gathered, were themselves political venues and potential sites of disorder. The censors saw themselves as guardians of public morality and had immense control over what subjects could be portrayed on stage. Censorship in Italy became particularly repressive after the revolutions of 1848, but varied from area to area. It tended to be most liberal in the north and most strict in the south, particularly in Naples and Rome. Verdi encountered particular difficulties whenever one of his works was performed in these cities.

Censorship worked in several ways. First the scenario for an opera and later its libretto were submitted to the censor for checking, who would demand that certain changes be made.

(Interestingly, the music came under little scrutiny, since it was not seen as being capable of conveying political messages.) Once the text had been given the all clear, the censors would do further checks in rehearsal and would then attend all performances, in order to make sure that performers sang the text as agreed and that they were not undermining the changes requested by the censor through gesture, tone or expression. Approval even had to be granted for the costumes the characters were to wear. Immodest dress would not have been tolerated anywhere, but in Risorgimento Rome and Naples the censors went so far as to ban costumes in red, green and white that made implicit reference to the Italian flag.

Operas could be censored on political grounds, on moral grounds or on religious grounds. Things that might seem completely harmless to us today were very often deemed shocking and unacceptable. Political censorship was particularly strict – subjects that showed disrespect to rulers or governments were banned, as were expressions of patriotism prior to the unification of Italy. Mentions of conspiracy or assassination were frowned upon, and banned by the strictest censors. Religious censorship not only entailed avoiding blasphemy, but also the use of seemingly innocuous words such as 'angel', 'heaven' or 'hell' – contorted alternatives had to be found. Phrases from the Bible were most certainly forbidden, along with anything that contradicted the authority of the Church. This meant that virtue must be emphasized at all times and some states went so far as to ban the depiction on stage of adultery, illegitimate children, assassination, murder or suicide. Such limitations were clearly frustrating for opera composers, for these topics are clearly the stuff of which many good dramas are made. Librettists were often forced to sanitize their libretti with meaningless, pompous language or alterations that were dramatically nonsensical, and audiences had to do their best to read between the lines to interpret the intended message.

Verdi had numerous battles with the censors, both when his operas were first written and when they were later revived in a number of different Italian cities. For example, censors put up objections to his opera *Stiffelio* (1850) just a matter of days before the first performance, objecting to a key scene where a story from the New Testament about an adulterous woman is read aloud (a reading that had obvious parallels with the heroine's own plight). His opera *Macbeth*, meanwhile, was deemed acceptable when it was first performed in Florence in 1847 but had to be performed in bowdlerized versions elsewhere. In Rome, for example, references to the supernatural had to be cut – gypsies were substituted for the three witches; while in Naples and Palermo references to the killing of kings had to be removed (undermining the central premise of the plot); and in Austrian-governed Milan, the chorus of oppressed Scots had to be given new words.

As noted above, later on in Verdi's career he was less preoccupied by politics and more by the psychology of human drama. His 1851 opera *Rigoletto* might seem at first glance to be little more than a tragic love story. However, it too infuriated the censors. The play upon which *Rigoletto* was based was Victor Hugo's *Le Roi s'amuse*, which had itself been banned in France for many years due to its perceived mockery of the nobility. Like Verdi himself, the dramatist, poet and playwright Hugo was actively involved in politics, serving as a member of parliament and a senator. And like Verdi, he too used his dramatic works as a vehicle for political messages, to speak out against social injustice and to criticize those in charge.

The central character in *Rigoletto* is a hunchbacked jester who works at the court of the corrupt, womanizing Duke of Mantua. Rigoletto joins in with the cruelty and mockery of the court and is cursed for doing so by the father of one of the women the Duke has seduced. Outside of the court, however, the private Rigoletto is a very different man, a good-hearted father devoted to his motherless daughter Gilda, whom he protectively keeps locked away except on the occasions when she is allowed to attend church. Unfortunately, on one of those occasions Gilda has encountered the Duke, who arranges for her to be kidnapped so that he can seduce her. Rigoletto cooks up a revenge plot by luring the Duke to the house of a hired assassin. But Gilda decides to sacrifice her own life in order to save the Duke, turning up at the assassin's house disguised as a young man.

Verdi found the Rigoletto subject highly appealing but realized from the outset that obtaining permission to set the work would be difficult. He wrote: 'I have in mind a subject that would be one of the greatest creations of the modern theatre if the police would only allow it. Who knows? They allowed *Ernani*, they might even allow us to do this and at least there are no conspiracies in it'. The first change Verdi was forced to make was in his chosen title for the opera – he wanted to call it *La maledizione* ('The Curse') – but this was deemed offensive to good taste. The censors in Venice, where the opera was to be first performed, then asked to see Piave's libretto, expressing concern about rumours they had heard about the original play's reception in France. After reading the libretto, they wrote back to say that they were horrified by the 'repulsive immorality and obscene triviality of the plot' and put an immediate ban on the setting of Hugo's story.

The censors particularly objected to the moral aspects of the story – the kidnapping, rape and murder of Gilda and the fact that the Duke goes unpunished. At a more detailed level they objected to certain words or references to religious terminology they found offensive. Clearly, the depiction of a ruler as licentious and corrupt was also highly problematic, as was the fact that the work showed a servant rising up against his master. Dead bodies were not allowed on stage and much objection was made to the fact that Gilda's dead body was dragged across the stage in a sack. The censors even objected to the fact that the central character was a hunchback – something Verdi deemed absolutely crucial, for one of the issues he wished to explore in the work was the tension between outer deformity and inner goodness.

Piave was forced to rewrite the libretto. His first version, entitled *Il duca di Vendôme*, pacified the censors but was unacceptable to Verdi because he felt that everything that was powerful about Hugo's play had been removed – the Duke was no longer depicted as a libertine, removing the very reason for the curse that drives the drama. Verdi made his objections clear in a letter to the president of the La Fenice opera house in Venice, justifying why certain scenes were fundamental to the drama, and concluding that 'in sum a powerful and original drama has been turned into something trivial and dead'. His letter was so persuasive that he managed to convince the censors to allow him to maintain many elements of the original story, and the second rewriting – as *Rigoletto* – satisfied both parties.

Nevertheless, Verdi and his librettist were forced to make certain compromises. The characters were kept from the original play but their names had to be changed, because Hugo's work was based on real historical characters. The action had to be moved from the court of François I to that of an anonymous Duke of Mantua. Composer and librettist were also forced to cut some of the more extreme libertine passages – Gilda's seduction, for example, had to take place offstage, whereas in the original version it was envisaged to take place in front of the audience. The ending to the opera also had to be made less macabre: Rigoletto grieves over his daughter's death alone, whereas in the play this scene takes place in front of a crowd of bypassers, including a doctor who examines the corpse.

Rigoletto's premiere in Venice was a great success. However, Verdi continued to have battles with the censor as the opera embarked upon its tour of the Italian states and later of the whole of Europe. In some cities, bastardized versions of the opera had to be performed, under different titles and with alterations to characters' names and to dramatic situations. In the first decade of the opera's history, well over a hundred productions were put on of the opera, but more often than not it was performed under a different name: *Viscardello*, *Lionello* and *Clara di Perth* were among the revised titles. As this last title would suggest, the action was often moved to settings extremely remote from those Verdi had intended: *Clara di Perth* was set in Scotland in order to capitalize on the success of recent operas inspired by the works of Walter Scott.

Some versions were highly incongruous, incorporating changes that meant the opera no longer made dramatic sense (for

OPERA CENSORSHIP TODAY

You might assume that censorship is no longer a problem for opera composers. We live in an age in which artistic freedom is almost limitless; indeed, shocking audiences through contemporary art is now almost run-of-the-mill. As we have seen, contemporary productions of established operas sometimes push the boundaries of taste to their limits. New works, too, tackle controversial topics, often based on episodes drawn from real life. For instance, John Adams's *The Death of Klinghoffer* (1991) deals with the hijacking of a cruise ship by Palestinian terrorists in 1985, during which a Jewish man in a wheelchair was thrown overboard. Thomas Adès's *Powder her Face* (1995) is based on the true story of a member of the British aristocracy who caused a scandal in the 1960s after a number of photographs of her in sexually explicit poses appeared during her divorce case. Although neither opera was 'censored', both provoked a public outcry, demonstrating that opera can still generate political debate. *The Death of Klinghoffer* was stridently criticized by prominent American musicologist Richard Taruskin and some Jewish groups have staged demonstrations against the work. *Powder her Face*, meanwhile, was banned, on account of explicit passages in its libretto, by the British radio station Classic FM.

instance, removing the scene in which Gilda is kidnapped). In others, the Duke was no longer shown as a libertine, or the heroine was wounded rather than killed at the end, in response to objections from the Church about the depiction of suicide on stage. One version, performed in Modena as *Viscardello*, ended with the Act Four Quartet, removing the storm, the stabbing, the final duet, Gilda's death and all dramatic tension. Verdi found the censorship battles that he faced deeply frustrating, feeling that many of the suggested changes had the potential profoundly to undermine his dramatic vision. He was often able to make a powerful case to the censors in order to get his own way to a large extent; however, there was little he could do about changes that were made to his operas when they were performed subsequently in different cities.

The politicization of opera

So far, this chapter has dealt primarily with operas that set political themes and in Chapter Two we saw that operas can become political through their stagings. However, operas may also be politicized by the ways in which they are interpreted by audiences, critics and other commentators, often going way beyond the intentions of their creators. Puccini presents an interesting paradox because he has often been presented as an 'apolitical' composer and yet his operas were strongly politicized in his own day. At the most basic level, Puccini has always polarized opinion. Shortly after his death, an Italian critic, Guido M. Gatti, said that: 'there has perhaps been no example, in the history of Italian music of the last fifty years, of an oeuvre that has provoked as much praise and as much hostility as that of Giacomo Puccini'. Why, then, did people feel so strongly about Puccini and everything for which he stood?

We have already seen that national identity was a burning topic in Verdi's Italy, and it continued to be so in Puccini's time. Italy had by now been politically unified for some decades, but the issue was still not done and dusted. Around the turn of the twentieth century it was still widely felt that there was little sense of a coherent cultural identity that all of the newly united Italians shared. Furthermore, there was a widely held belief in turn-of-the-century Italy that the nation was in a period of social and moral decline. Puccini's works became dragged into these arguments, despite the fact that he had no interest in becoming actively involved in politics and cared little about political debate.

The turn of the twentieth century was a time when all European nations were anxiously but aggressively asserting their national identities. As we have already seen, the arts were intimately linked to debates about patriotism, and in Italy opera was a particularly useful nationalistic tool, as an art-form that had been invented there and exported with great success to the rest of the world. It was inevitable that Puccini, as the most prominent Italian opera composer of his day, should have got dragged into the debate, but responses to him were extremely mixed. On the one hand his supporters held him and his music up as the antidote to all of the nation's cultural problems. On the other, his detractors presented them as the embodiment of everything that was wrong with contemporary Italian art and society. Puccini's operas therefore became embroiled in debates about all sorts of non-musical issues, from empire and race to gender. Critics of Puccini's own time pointed again and again to the connections that they perceived between his operas and developments in contemporary society: the works thus became political, irrespective of their composer's own lack of interest in politics.

So why did Puccini's operas become so politicized, as opposed to those of his contemporaries such as Mascagni or

Leoncavallo? Well, Puccini was thrust into the limelight early on in his career and effectively elected by the contemporary press and musical establishment to take on the role of successor to Verdi (Verdi and Puccini shared a powerful publisher, Ricordi). This position was a vital and highly contested one. As we have seen, the Italian operatic tradition was thought to be something that could bring the Italian people together, yet this tradition was itself perceived to be under threat. Italian opera had to reposition itself and reinvent itself in the face of a challenge it faced from a 'new kid on the block' – German opera. German opera seemed to threaten everything that Italian opera stood for, yet Wagner's music and his theories about music were impossible to ignore. Many young Italian composers, keen to be seen as modern, started to imitate Wagner's compositional style. There was also an influx of French operas onto the Italian stage from the 1860s, which threw the Italian music press into a state of great panic. Politically speaking, Italy was now freed from foreign domination, yet in terms of culture it seem more enslaved to other nations than ever. This was extremely troubling: artistic productivity was regarded as something intimately connected to the 'health' of the nation, and musical decline was seen by many as a reflection of the wider social and political anxieties that Italy seemed to face. Italy needed a national composer to succeed Verdi around whose music the nation might rally. The man chosen for the job was Puccini.

In order to present Puccini as the answer to all of Italy's social and political problems, his publishers and supporters in the press wrote about him in the most grandiose of ways. They disseminated certain myths about Puccini's 'Italianness' that, in some cases, had very little to do with music. These focused upon his struggle against poverty, the fact that he came from a musical family and the fact that he came from Tuscany, an area that occupied a particularly significant place in the popular Italian imagination. Throughout Puccini's lifetime his works would be depicted as representative of the Italian climate and landscape. However, such emotive references were hardly ever supported by reference to specific aspects of the score.

Critics also wrote about Puccini using classical terminology, describing him as if he were a classical statue or emperor in order to draw a connection with Italy's glorious Roman past. At the same time, Puccini was presented as the embodiment of everything that was dynamic and modern: he was often depicted enjoying one of his favourite hobbies – driving fast cars. The composer was portrayed simultaneously as a glamorous international star and as a humble man of the people. Critics would continue to churn out the same well-worn anecdotes about Puccini until the very end of his life, depicting him metaphorically as a warrior, a classical statue, an everyman figure or as the descendent of an ancient race. However, by this time – the early years of the Fascist era – references to warriors and descendants of a 'pure' race had started to take on a darker twist.

But, of course, Puccini's mythologization at the hands of his supporters is only one side of this story. Now I'd like to turn this around and look at the other side of the coin – a critic who attacked Puccini vehemently, who saw him as the embodiment of all of Italy's problems rather than the solution to them. A damning book was published in 1912 entitled *Giacomo Puccini e l'opera internazionale* by a young musicologist called Fausto Torrefranca. Torrefranca made no attempt to disguise his disdain for the composer promoted by Ricordi as Verdi's successor. He wrote that 'Puccini ... embodies, with the utmost completeness, all the decadence of current Italian music, and represents all its cynical commercialism, all its pitiful impotence and the whole triumphant vogue for internationalism'. He claimed that Puccini's music was not Italian at all, portraying it as having been cobbled together from bits and pieces of music he had pinched from foreign composers, accusing him of writing a sort of musical 'Esperanto'.

Furthermore, Torrefranca brought other issues into the debate to try and blacken Puccini's name. For instance, he depicted Puccini as a 'feminized' composer, a label with harmful political implications and in complete contrast to the image of the strong, manly Puccini his patrons had tried to create. He used metaphorical language in order to launch a series of insults at Puccini – calling his music weak, sick and unoriginal – all of which were intended to reinforce the composer's supposed 'effeminacy'. To associate Puccini with women was an insult, since women were still widely portrayed at the turn of the twentieth century by male artists and thinkers as being incapable of any form of significant artistic creativity. Torrefranca continued his diatribe by associating Puccini with other groups within society who were considered at the time to be 'outsiders', including homosexuals and Jews. This was all part of a strategy to undermine the image of Puccini as a strong, manly 'national' composer.

Torrefranca's attack on Puccini was motivated by a complex mix of political, social and cultural prejudices. His right-wing, anti-democratic views shaped his attitude towards music: he believed that true art was something that could only be appreciated by a small, intellectual elite, so it is unsurprising that he was ill-disposed to Puccini's brand of crowd-pleasing opera. It is tempting to dismiss his comments as the ravings of a bigoted eccentric. However, the extra-musical remarks he made about Puccini can tell us much about debates that were taking place about national identity in the lead-up to the advent of Fascism in Italy. Moreover, there is evidence to suggest that some other music critics shared his views about Puccini, and some of Torrefranca's criticisms of Puccini's compositional ability even paved the way for the hostility and snobbery about the composer's music that can still be found within the musicological establishment today. What should be obvious from this brief summary is that Puccini's music prompted very strong feelings during his lifetime, and that the debates surrounding it lay at the heart of a crisis of national identity that was gripping Italy. Politics were a key part of Puccini's reception history, despite his own relative lack of interest in political matters. Although aspects of Puccini's works still seem political today (his treatment of women and his representation of other cultures, for instance, which will be discussed further in the next chapter), his works are less frequently associated today with debates about Italian national identity. Let's turn now to a composer who was both political in his own time and whose works prompt equally fraught political debates today.

Wagner and anti-Semitism

One of the most famous cases in which opera and politics seem to collide is that of Richard Wagner. In the popular imagination it has become received wisdom that Wagner was a right-wing, nationalistic anti-Semite, whose works have become tainted by association with the Nazis. However, this is a much more complicated matter than it might at first seem. For a start, Wagner's personal political identity was complex and in some respects is difficult to map on to contemporary notions of 'left' and 'right': during his youth he could justifiably be considered to have been something of a revolutionary, and associated with artistic liberals and even political radicals. Wagner believed passionately in social reform and in the idea that art should be freed from capitalism and financial profit – the idea that society itself should be reinvented as much as art lies at the heart of his theoretical works such as *Art and Revolution* (*Die Kunst und die Revolution*, 1849). At this time, in fact, nationalism was a cause associated more with the left than with the right: Wagner wished to reject traditional social hierarchies and envisaged a new Germany based upon folk culture, with peasants living together in a utopian society.

If it is possible to challenge the image of Wagner as a far-right extremist, it is more difficult to refute charges against him of anti-Semitism. In 1850 he wrote an essay entitled *Das Judenthum in der Musik* (*Judaism in Music*), in which he argued that Jews were responsible for all the most undesirable developments in modern music. Wagner developed theories about Jewish attempts to speak foreign languages, which he then extended to their efforts in musical composition. (Torrefranca, incidentally, borrowed some of these ideas for his book on Puccini. The fact that Puccini was not Jewish was irrelevant: Torrefranca hoped to associate Puccini with Jews in order to undermine his status as national composer.) Wagner suggested that Jews had no musical language of their own, no independent ideas, and that they merely borrowed the musical language of those amongst whom they dwelled. The result, in Wagner's opinion, was a musical style that was eclectic and had no identity of its own – he accused Jewish composers of taking the best of the various national styles they encountered and turning out works which were superficially attractive but essentially meaningless. Furthermore, drawing upon clichés linking Jews with money-making, he associated them with the profit-driven musical culture that he so detested. Some have speculated that Wagner wanted to ridicule contemporary Jewish composers such as Mendelssohn and Meyerbeer, whose popular success he envied.

While such ideas may seem abhorrent to us, they would not – unfortunately – have seemed so strange to Wagner's contemporary readership, merely tapping into an anti-Semitic mindset that had been deeply ingrained, even normalized, in German society (and elsewhere in Europe) for centuries. It was common for middle-class intellectuals who considered themselves liberals to hold anti-Semitic views. To say that Wagner was 'of his time' is not to make excuses for him – merely to point out that as anti-Semitism was widespread in Europe during the nineteenth century, we should not be surprised to find that Wagner held anti-Semitic views. Indeed, he was not the only well-known nineteenth-century cultural figure to have held such opinions – Schumann, for instance, is often cited as having made anti-Semitic remarks about Mendelssohn, as is painter Pierre-Auguste Renoir about his contemporary Camille Pissarro. The difference was that Wagner's anti-Semitism extended beyond off-the-cuff personal remarks to going so far as to write what amounted to an anti-Semitic manifesto, which even shocked and embarrassed some of his friends when it was reissued under his name in 1869 (it had originally been published anonymously).

Although much of Wagner's anti-Semitism seems to have stemmed from jealousy of Jewish composers whom he perceived to be enjoying an 'unfair' degree of success when he was struggling in poverty during the early years of his career, it sometimes took on a darker tone. He also set up a journal, the *Bayreuther Blätter*, conceived to address the question of the perceived 'decline of the species'. Articles appeared in the journal overtly asserting that racial mixing of Jews and non-Jews had corrupted humanity, an idea that might seem directly to pre-empt the eugenicist arguments put forward by the Nazis. Crucially, however, while Wagner suggested that Jews could be 're-educated' (in part through his own works!) he never advocated violence towards the Jewish people, stopping far short of the 'solutions' to the 'Jewish problem' put forward by the Nazis. Indeed, he had many Jewish friends and associates, and the ideas he promoted about the purity of the Aryan race were becoming highly fashionable in Germany in the later years of his life – Wagner was by no means unusual in speaking about these ideas.

In assessing Wagner's anti-Semitism, we might consider his operatic works in addition to his theoretical writings. Here things become more complicated. Many scholars have pointed to instances in selected Wagner operas that seem to stage his ideological theories about the Jewish race. (These arguments are, of course, based primarily on a reading of the libretti for the works in question: it is more difficult – although arguably not impossible – to argue convincingly that music can be 'racist' or indeed political in any way.) Some scholars have argued that the character Beckmesser in Wagner's *The Mastersingers of Nuremberg* (*Die Meistersinger von Nürnberg*) is an anti-Semitic caricature. This comic work tells the story of a tradesman's guild of mastersingers in sixteenth-century Nuremberg. The guild has its own long-established traditions, one of which is to hold regular singing competitions, in which participants must perform songs that correspond with a strict set of pre-existing guidelines. Sixtus Beckmesser is the town clerk and one of two mastersingers competing for the hand of a young woman called Eva, whose father has promised her to the winner of the singing competition (Eva prefers Beckmesser's rival, Walther von Stolzing). Beckmesser is represented as a singer who cobbles together musical styles to create works that are unattractive. The music Wagner gives to him is often deliberately ungainly, discordant, awkwardly embellished and sits uncomfortably within his bass vocal range. When Beckmesser attempts to sing the prize song, he gets the words wrong and makes a mess of the music: the song is garbled, like Jewish attempts to speak foreign languages, according to Wagner's theory. He is not a real artist, Wagner suggests, but merely an imitation of one. The links with Wagner's theories on Jewish musical language are self-evident.

There is a pronounced element of Christian imagery in the opera – Walther is effectively 'baptized' at the end and can be read as a Christ-like figure who has come to 'redeem' art. Beckmesser is positioned as an outsider to this tradition. Some scholars have suggested that, once again, a real person was the specific butt of Wagner's anti-Semitic caricature. In this case it was the critic Eduard Hanslick (whose mother was Jewish, although he had converted to Catholicism), who had been critical of Wagner's more recent works. So we could consider whether the creation of the Beckmesser character was an attack on Jews more generally, or perhaps merely an attempt to lampoon a particular individual – although we might find this idea equally offensive. Some scholars have suggested that characters who appear to be anti-Semitic stereotypes can also be found in the Ring and *Parsifal*, and ideas of racial purity are a common theme throughout Wagner's works. However, Wagner never categorically stated that he intended to create a Jewish caricature in one of his works, and one might argue that interpreting these characters as Jewish is no more than that – an interpretation. It is interesting to note that a far more overt Jewish caricature can be found in the figure of Shylock in Shakespeare's *The Merchant of Venice*, yet it is uncommon to find Shakespeare being accused of anti-Semitism.

If the suspicion that Wagner was anti-Semitic rested solely on his prose works and (possible) allusions in his operas, it is highly unlikely that the general public at large would draw any parallels between the composer and anti-Semitism. The fact that they do so stems from something else entirely: the perceived appropriation of Wagner by the Nazis. Wagner is often regarded as '*the* Nazi composer', but is this fair? There is a school of thought that Hitler derived his anti-Semitic views from Wagner's writings, but as Wagner's writings were merely part of a broader nineteenth-century discourse on Jews and on racial purity, this claim is difficult to prove categorically. Bryan Magee has argued that Hitler's hatred of Jews seems to have stemmed primarily from his hatred of socialists (some of whom were also Jewish), whom he blamed for allowing Germany to fall into chaos after the First World War. Thus, one might argue that Hitler's brand of anti-Semitism was politically derived whereas Wagner's was culturally focused. Again, this is not in any sense to make excuses for Wagner, but simply to argue that any attempt to try to draw a causal link between Wagner's writings (let alone his music) and the horrors of the Holocaust would be simplistic.

Hitler saw in Wagner's works a shared vision of an ideal Germany and was certainly passionate about Wagner's music, commissioning performances of Wagner's works for special occasions. However, it would not be accurate to say that Wagner was the only composer favoured by the Nazi regime: the music of other canonical composers was much performed and promoted in Germany during the Third Reich, and has not been stigmatized as a result. As Shirli Gilbert has shown, Wagner's music was played in the Nazi concentration camps by orchestras made up of inmates, for the enjoyment of the SS, but so too was music by composers as diverse as Beethoven, Mozart, Bizet, Verdi and Tchaikovsky.

Nevertheless, Wagner is still often held up as being in some sense 'guilty by association', but there are a number of counts on which we might challenge this concept. Wagner was, of course, not alive by the time the Nazis came to power (indeed, he died six years before Adolf Hitler was born). Therefore he did not give his consent to the Nazis' appropriation of his music, and there is no way we can know what he would have made of such an appropriation or whether he would have condoned the Nazis' actions. Since Wagner has no voice with which to defend himself, it is arguably rather problematic to make anachronistic assumptions about him and to project back onto him associations and interpretations that make sense to us but which would have meant nothing to him.

However, so strong is the feeling that Wagner is in some sense intertwined with the Third Reich that performances of his works have been banned in Israel, in order to avoid offending Holocaust survivors. The Jewish, Argentinian-born conductor Daniel Barenboim has faced strong opposition when he has tried to introduce excerpts from Wagner's works into concert programmes when visiting Israel. Barenboim has stated that 'Wagner, the person, is absolutely appalling, despicable', and called the composer's anti-Semitism 'monstrous'. What is interesting is that he finds these personal qualities he attributes to the composer difficult to reconcile with the noble, uplifting qualities he discerns in the music. For Barenboim then, the man and the music can be separated – and the music deserves to be heard. Others would doubtless disagree. The arguments about Wagner's anti-Semitism will almost certainly rage on and on, but it is worth thinking about the following questions. Is anti-Semitism somehow 'ingrained' in Wagner's music? Can we separate out the music from the man whose views we find so abhorrent? Should we ban or boycott his music? Or is it ridiculous to make Wagner 'guilty by association'?

As we have seen, operas from the past engaged directly with the important political issues of the day. Today, opera occupies a less prominent place in society and it is less easy to see opera as a political force. However, contemporary operas continue to engage with the topic of politics, as the discussion of works by Adès and Adams above demonstrated. (Other recent operas on political topics include Adams's *Nixon in China* (1985–7) and Philip Glass's opera *Satyagraha* (1979), which focuses upon Mahatma Gandhi's formative years in South Africa.) Furthermore, some of the political messages inherent in operas from the past can still speak powerfully to us today. Let's turn now to thinking about two issues that, by and large, did not trouble audiences in the past, but which seem deeply political to present-day audiences: gender and race.

4

Opera and identity: gender and race

This chapter continues looking at opera and politics in the broad sense of the word, focusing on the two themes of gender and race. In recent decades, scholars have started to take an interest in how issues of gender relate to music: this field of interest developed out of feminist scholarship in other disciplines such as literature. Although gendered or feminist approaches have been applied to many different types of music (Susan McClary, for instance, has written about gendered narratives in symphonic works), opera clearly lends itself particularly easily to this sort of approach because it is music with a text and characters. Race and empire are also topics that have started to interest opera historians in recent decades, influenced by the 'post-colonial' approaches that have been developed by scholars in other Humanities disciplines. Recent changes in thinking about gender and race within both academia and society more broadly mean that many operas from the nineteenth century and earlier are being reappraised today. Issues and themes that would probably not have drawn comment at the time when the opera in question was written may seem deeply controversial nowadays. However, there is a debate to be had here about the extent to which we ought to judge art-works from the past by the moral standards of the present.

Suffering heroines

Feminism has become an important concern within musicology since the 1980s, with a growing number of scholars (female and male) starting to investigate the neglected role of women – whether as composers or performers – in the history of music. Scholars have asked why women musicians have historically been excluded from what is often referred to as the musical 'canon' (a body of works and composers frequently held up as being particularly significant). They have questioned the idea – widely held in previous centuries – that women are incapable of meaningful artistic endeavour, recuperating the music of long-forgotten female composers or demonstrating the social and political reasons why women in the past were prevented from fulfilling their creative potential. Those women who were allowed to compose in previous centuries were often steered towards small-scale genres of music associated with domestic settings, such as chamber music or song: few had the opportunity to try their hand at large-scale musical genres such as the symphony or opera. Of course, there were exceptions to this rule and more and more opportunities began to open up for women in the twentieth century (see p. 109). However, the vast majority of operas throughout history that have gained widespread public recognition have been composed by men, and in recent years scholars have investigated the impact this male monopoly of the art-form has had upon the portrayal of women in opera. One prominent line of thought in recent opera scholarship has been that many operas from the past place great emphasis on the suffering of women, and were arguably shaped by agendas that were detrimental to women. Let's begin by examining the case for this argument.

While there are many male operatic characters who suffer and die, it would certainly be true to say that they are

WOMEN OPERA COMPOSERS

Although few women throughout history have been given the opportunity to compose operas (or to have their operas performed) there have been some notable exceptions. The earliest known female opera composer was Francesca Caccini, who was born in Florence in 1587. She was closely involved with the earliest opera composers: she sang in the first performance of Peri's *Euridice*, knew Monteverdi and married a member of the Florentine Camerata. In time, she became a composer herself, writing a number of operas for the Medici court, although only one survives. Several centuries on, the early twentieth-century British composer Ethel Smyth was one of very few female composers of her day to write in the large forms of opera, oratorio and concerto. Her most famous opera was *The Wreckers*, which tells the story of the residents of a Cornish village who lure ships to their destruction on the rocks so as to plunder their cargo. It was first performed in Germany in 1906, wasn't taken up in Smyth's native Britain for a further three years, and was never accepted into the operatic canon. Today there are fewer barriers to female creativity, and successful contemporary figures within the field of opera include the Finnish composer Kaija Saariaho and the British composer Judith Weir.

outnumbered by their bruised and bullied lovers, sisters and daughters. Indeed, if we think of the popular nineteenth-century works that still dominate the repertory at many opera houses today, it is hard to think of a female protagonist in a serious opera who is not subjected to psychological torment followed by an unpleasant death. (There are, of course, a few exceptions – the heroine of Tchaikovsky's *Eugene Onegin*, for example, is tragic in a different way.) Many operatic heroines are seduced and abandoned innocents with little control over their destinies, and those bold few who try to turn the tables and have a good time along the way, such as Carmen, invariably come to regret it. One might go so far as to suggest that the ill-treatment of women is a fundamental driving force behind nineteenth-century opera. In recent years scholars have begun to question why this should be, to consider why cruelty to women should ever have been deemed good entertainment, and to ask how witnessing such acts makes us feel as twenty-first-century viewers.

Virtually all heroines of nineteenth- and early twentieth-century operas are killed off at the end, many in extremely violent circumstances. Some of the more gruesome operatic deaths include that of Fenella in Auber's *La Muette de Portici*, who jumps into the erupting mouth of Mount Vesuvius, or Rachel, the heroine of Halévy's *La Juive* (1835), who is thrown into a vat of boiling oil. Both of these are French Grand Operas from the early nineteenth century, in which stage spectacle was considered highly important. These ultra-dramatic deaths, which are potentially difficult to stage, would have contributed to the 'spectacular' excess of these works. Other operatic deaths are either improbable or downright bizarre: Mascagni's *Iris* (1898) throws herself into a sewer and Cilea's *Adriana Lecouvreur* (1902) dies after smelling a bunch of poisoned violets. It might seem that an opera from this period would not be an opera without the death of the heroine – this was a dramatic convention that nineteenth-century audiences expected. Sometimes, when a literary work being adapted as an opera did not feature a female death, the librettist altered it so as to include one. In Puccini's *Turandot*, for example, the eponymous heroine does not die and is (reluctantly) united with the hero. But Puccini and his librettists invented another character – the slave girl Liù – who does not feature in the original literary source (a play by the eighteenth-century dramatist Carlo Gozzi), who commits suicide in order to save the hero, whom she loves but who plainly does not love her. Interestingly – as Puccini and his

librettists perhaps suspected – the audience loved the sentimental, self-sacrificing Liù rather than the hard-hearted Turandot,
but her inclusion in the opera could be said to be rather
gratuitous.

However, if we are going to point the finger at opera for
treating female characters cruelly, we must do the same for other
forms of art. In the nineteenth century in particular, women and
death were inextricably fused in cultural artefacts, with novels,
paintings and stage works taking the dying woman as a potent
source of inspiration. As Edgar Allen Poe wrote in *The
Philosophy of Composition* (1846), 'The death of a beautiful
woman is, unquestionably, the most poetical topic in the world'.
The heroine's sacrifice was often a prerequisite for the hero's
redemption, and dead women were even used as an allegory for
the creative act itself. The pursuit by mortal men of spectral
female spirits in such ballets as *La Sylphide* (1832) and *Giselle*
(1841), for instance, symbolized the ceaseless quest of the
Romantic artist for the unattainable. In painting, one might
point to a veritable cult of dead or dying women: pre-
Raphaelite artist John Everett Millais's celebrated painting of the
drowned Ophelia is just one example of a painter fetishizing the
beautiful dead female body.

It is interesting to note that if we look back at seventeenth-
and eighteenth-century operas, it is possible to find a broader
spectrum of female character types, including powerful heroines,
and a tragic ending was not a prerequisite for a serious opera.
However, nineteenth-century gender politics dealt in black and
white clichés: a woman was either Mary or Eve, an angel or a
whore. In the early to mid nineteenth century, women were
often represented – whether in operas, paintings or literary
works – as angelic or redemptive figures. However, this taste for
passive, gentle figures gave way to a more realistic, sometimes
brutal depiction of transgressive women by the later nineteenth
century. Sexually confident or independent women were

perceived to be a threat to social order and had to be punished to reinforce their position in society at that time. Nineteenth-century art-works were highly didactic, a useful moral tool for upholding the respectable bourgeois status quo, policing gendered behaviour and controlling women's sexuality. The middle-class woman's mission was to be a devoted wife and mother and her life beyond the home was strictly circumscribed. Any transgression from this path would result in social condemnation, and art-works were often used to show what would happen to those who strayed.

A particularly popular topic in nineteenth-century culture was the fallen woman with a 'heart of gold', a theme that was all the rage in mid-century French literature. These generous, warm-hearted girls were forced by unfortunate social circumstances into a life of vice and then 'purified' by the love of a good man. Readers avidly followed their plight in serialized newspaper instalments; among the most adored were Fleur-de-Marie, the central figure in Eugène Sue's immensely popular *Les Mystères de Paris* (1842–1843), and Esther in Balzac's *Splendeurs et misères des courtisanes* (1847). Respectable bourgeois men naturally wanted their wives to be paragons of virtue, but the loose woman also exercised a dangerous fascination which artists and writers were quick to exploit. However, society's conventions dictated that these characters be killed off – usually by an unpleasant disease symbolizing their 'contamination' of decent society – for the fallen woman, however sentimentalized, could never be allowed to triumph.

The most famous operatic treatment of this subject was Verdi's *La traviata* (1853), based upon Alexandre Dumas's play *La Dame aux camélias*, which in turn was based upon an earlier novel he had written. The courtesan Violetta (whom Dumas calls Marguerite) is 'purified' when the hero Alfredo (Armand in Dumas's version) falls in love with her, and transports her to a new life in the countryside. However, Alfredo's father Germont persuades Violetta to leave, fearing for the good name of his unmarried daughter (Alfredo's sister, a character we do not meet). Violetta does so, and later dies of consumption, and Alfredo and his father are filled with remorse. The heroine is therefore literally sacrificed in order to preserve the respectability of the family unit.

However, Verdi's interpretation of these events was very different to those of Dumas. Dumas's original autobiographical novel of 1848 was based upon an affair he had had with the courtesan Marie Duplessis. In the novel, the hero (Dumas's alter ego) seems to take pleasure in tormenting his heroine. He condemns her to a life where she is isolated both from her old world and from the respectable community she has attempted to join, and then allows her to die sad, alone and in pain. As a final twist, he has her body exhumed, a ghoulish scene which, for obvious reasons of moral propriety, was omitted when the novel was adapted as a play in 1852. Verdi's treatment of the subject is much more humane: he depicts his heroine (now Italianized as Violetta) as the most rather than the least moral figure in the opera, and treats her death with compassion rather than voyeurism.

Here, then, we have a rare example of a composer who presents the age-old archetype of woman as victim, but makes his disapproval clear. Verdi was particularly drawn to this subject because of the parallels he could see between Violetta's plight and the way in which his own partner, Giuseppina Strepponi, had been treated. (Verdi and Strepponi, who was a singer, lived together for over a decade before marrying in 1859. She had several illegitimate children from a previous relationship and was ostracized by members of Verdi's home town in Italy.) However, one might argue that not all composers were as compassionate to their heroines as Verdi. Puccini in particular has a reputation for treating them sadistically. The heroine of his 1904 opera *Madama Butterfly*, Cio-Cio San, is referred to in the libretto as a butterfly which the hero will pursue even at the risk of damaging its wings. Butterfly seems to be emblematic of the destiny of almost all women in nineteenth-century opera: to be fragile and ornamental playthings, victims of the selfish and destructive impulses of men. But there are other ways in which we might look at Puccini's treatment of women, and some of these may cast his motives in a less negative light. I shall return to this opera presently, as it raises interesting questions about my twin themes of gender and race. Firstly, let's take a look at what scholars have said about the treatment of women in opera.

Recent interpretations

During earlier centuries, the treatment of women in operas would often have gone without comment or question, but since the advent of feminism, we tend to view this issue rather differently. A ground-breaking text in the debate about operatic heroines was *Opera, or the Undoing of Women* by the French feminist literary critic Catherine Clément, first published in 1979 and translated into English in 1988. Clément analyses the plots of over thirty well-known operas in a bid to demonstrate to the opera-lover the negative messages about women that are being presented in these works. Clément's thesis is that all women in opera are victims – whether they are murdered or simply have the life sucked out of them.

Clément's book is angry and polemical and written in a highly poetic, idiosyncratic style. It has attracted both praise and criticism from reviewers and musicologists. It is difficult to dispute her case that a lot of heroines die and suffer in opera, but her book has been criticized on a number of counts. Where her thesis becomes particularly controversial is where she starts to draw connections between nineteenth-century operas and

Those who die poisoned, gently; those who are choked; those who fold in on themselves peaceful. Violent deaths, lyrical deaths, gentle deaths, talkative or silent deaths ..... Nine by knife, two of them suicides; three by fire; two who jump; two consumptives; three who drown; three poisoned; two of fright; and a few unclassifiable, thank god for them, dying without anyone knowing why or how. Still, that is just the first sorting. And with my nice clean slate in my hands, I examine all those dream names in their pigeonholes, like butterflies spread out on boards. All that is left is to write their names above them: Violetta, Mimì, Gilda, Norma, Brunhilde, Senta, Antonia, Marfa .... The frightened, pathetic exercise of taxonomic intelligence, reassuring itself by filling its sensible little categories. But no matter how hard I laugh, there is always this constant: death by a man. Whether they do it themselves, like Butterfly, or are stabbed, like Carmen, the provenance of the knife, or the choking hand, or the fading breath is a man, and the result is fatal.

Catherine Clément: *Opera, or the Undoing of Women*
(Virago, 1989), p. 47

contemporary society: she depicts what happens in operas as merely an extension of what happens in real life:

Plain and simple, just like real life. Like all pictures this one only brings out something obvious – something that was present in reality; that is how life is. Was this detour in capital letters necessary, or this display of music in all its magnificent splendor, just to lay low centuries of oppression and domesticity? So what is this pleasure in opera; what is perverse about it? And this durability (whereas the form has been dead for nearly half a century) – what is it linked to? What awarenesses dimmed by beauty and the sublime come to stand in the darkness of the hall and watch the infinitely repetitive spectacle of a woman who dies, murdered?

(Clément, p. 47)

In other words, Clément contends, opera tells a tale of male domination and female oppression, which she regards as common to most artistic products of West European nineteenth-century culture. However, she suggests that it does so more explicitly and more seductively than other art-forms because the music, in its beauty, anaesthetizes us to the terrible events that unfold before our eyes in much-loved operas. 'Oh voices, sublime voices, high, clear voices', she writes, 'how you make one forget the words you sing!' Her argument that opera permits men to give voice to and act out an ingrained homicidal misogyny (albeit in disguised or distorted form) has been criticized for being extreme, simplistic and even offensive.

Beyond its capacity to alienate male readers, Clément's critique might be challenged at a number of other levels. To start with, there is, of course, a bigger picture. As several writers and reviewers have pointed out, Clément ignores women in comic operas, who often exact revenge upon or outwit foolish male characters or are the most cunning, clever characters in the opera (one thinks, for example, of Susanna in *Figaro*). Furthermore, one might make the obvious point that serious operas tend to deal with tragic situations and that tragedies, by their very nature, tend to involve death and suffering. Most crucially, perhaps, Clément's book has been criticized for largely ignoring the music of the operas she purports to analyse. As a literary theorist rather than a musicologist, she scrutinizes the operas purely at the level of plot. So, you might say, have I done so far, but I am prepared to acknowledge that this raises a problem. Opera is a multi-faceted art-form in which the music is far from being insignificant. If you take the music out, you might as well be analysing a play or a film. To ignore the music is to ignore a huge part of what makes an opera an opera: music is essential to how an opera communicates.

In fact, looking beyond the plots of operas to their music might offer some more encouraging perspectives on the representation of women in opera. We might argue that the music does not necessarily collude in the victimisation of the female characters. Indeed, some scholars have argued that the vocal prowess and physical virtuosity of operatic heroines grants them the empowerment, vitality and independence that they are denied by the plot. In a critique of Clément's book published in the *New York Times* in 1989, Paul Robinson argued that Clément would have been well advised to pay attention to the music because it is through this that the female characters attain parity with the men:

> Perhaps the single most important musical fact about opera's female victims is that they sing with an authority equal to that of their male oppressors. Opera is built on one of the great natural equalities, namely, the equality of men's and women's voices. Women can sing as loudly as men, their voices embrace as large a range as those of men and they have the advantage of commanding the heights where they can emit sounds of unparalleled incisiveness. They also enjoy greater vocal facility than men, thus allowing them to convey a sense of tremendous energy. In no other purely physical respect are women so clearly on a par with men. The world of sport – in many ways quite similar to opera in its physical demands – remains, by contrast, thoroughly segregated. This fundamental vocal fact (and the music it allows operatic composers to write for the female voice) means that women in opera are rarely experienced as victims. Rather, they seem subversive presences in a patriarchal culture, since they so manifestly contain the promise – or rather the threat – of women's full equality.
>
> (Paul Robinson, 'It's not over until the soprano dies', *New York Times*, 1 January 1989)

Finally, it is worth remembering that it is the heroines, on the whole, that we particularly love to hear in operas. These are the characters we really care about and who demand our sympathy, and it is almost invariably the *prima donna* who receives the longest and most enthusiastic applause at the end of an opera.

The issue of suffering heroines is just one facet of gender studies within opera. In recent years, scholars have tried to find more subtle ways of thinking about gender in opera. Some are still concerned with issues of representation (of men as well as women), and in finding ways of discussing the music in meaningful ways so as to shed light on gender issues. Others have borrowed interesting approaches from other Humanities disciplines in order to explore the ways in which we respond to the depiction of gender in opera. One fruitful approach has been to explore the idea of the 'gaze', a term borrowed from critical theory, which involves examining how spectators, whether male or female, look at and respond to female characters being depicted in opera, as a way of understanding gendered power relations. Another approach has been to draw upon theories of 'the body' and even to scrutinize operas in terms of their depiction of disease (which has sometimes stood as a metaphor for other, gendered, concerns). Finally, some scholars have questioned our assumptions about traditional gender roles by exploring operas where gender identities are blurred, for example the many works that use trouser roles ('male' roles played by female singers – a good example would be Cherubino in Mozart's *The Marriage of Figaro*). Overall, the field of gender studies within opera continues to expand, becoming ever more creative in its approaches and informing 'mainstream' operatic history to a greater and greater degree. Let's now turn to thinking about another expanding area of opera studies.

Opera and imperialism

Just as some musicologists have been influenced by feminist approaches from across the Humanities, they have also started to take an interest in post-colonial theories in recent years. Post-colonialism had established itself as an area of debate in such fields as literature and art history by the 1980s. Just as feminist scholars have been motivated by a desire to expose and challenge situations and art-works in which women have been excluded or subordinated by men, post-colonialist scholars have sought to illustrate the way in which Western culture has tended to view the world as being organized in terms of 'the self' (i.e. Western society, historically implicitly taken as the norm) and 'the Other'. Post-colonial scholars have demonstrated that artists and scholars in the past often posited this relationship as one between the colonizer and the colonized, resulting in patronizing depictions of non-Western societies. One consequence of the spread of these debates to musicology has been the rise of ethnomusicology. In the case of the study of classical music, post-colonial theories are most easily and logically applied to the many operas that take place in non-Western settings. But whereas ethnomusicologists adopt an anthropological approach, and deal with genuine musical practices from cultures other than their own, classical musicologists who are interested in musical 'exoticism' are primarily concerned with scrutinizing fantasy versions of non-Western music and non-Western cultures dreamed up by Western artists.

As far back as the seventeenth century, composers were attracted by the dramatic possibilities of writing 'exotic' operas set in distant locales, although they varied in the extent to which they attempted to match location and scenery with non-Western-sounding music. Turkey was a locale that proved particularly inspiring to early opera composers – there was a vogue in mid seventeenth-century Venice for patriotic operas about Venetian clashes with the Ottoman Empire. Continuing the Turkish theme, from the late eighteenth century we could point to Mozart's *Die Entführung aus dem Serail* – 'The Abduction from the Harem'. (The Turkish influence was also apparent in instrumental music – think of Mozart's famous piano work 'Rondo alla Turca'.) Of course, what constituted 'exotic' depended upon your own cultural identity. To early nineteenth-century Italian audiences, the mists and mountains evoked by Donizetti's Scottish opera *Lucia di Lammermoor* would have seemed highly romantic, and they doubtless thought that the same composer's *Emilia di Liverpool* sounded pretty exotic too, comical as it may sound to modern ears. Susan McClary has argued convincingly that Bizet took an 'oriental' approach in writing the music for the heroine of his Spanish opera *Carmen*. Spain may not strike us as a particularly 'oriental' location but in the preface to his *Les Orientales* (1829), Victor Hugo defined the realm of the Orient as including Spain, which he referred to as 'half African'. McClary has shown that Bizet used musical devices in *Carmen* which were similar to those used in operas set further afield, and can be interpreted as a 'code' that was used to depict the 'Orient'.

So, in a sense, anything that was different to your own culture could count as 'exotic'. But for the most part, we take operatic 'exoticism' to denote operas set in locations outside of Europe, places that the French, Italian, or German composers of the works in question in most cases never visited. By the nineteenth and early twentieth centuries there were scores of operas set in Middle or Far Eastern locales: Verdi's *Aida* (Egypt), Delibes's *Lakmé* (India), Bizet's *Les Pêcheurs des perles* (Ceylon, now Sri Lanka), Strauss's *Salome* (ancient Palestine), and Puccini's *Madama Butterfly* (Japan) and *Turandot* (China) are just the most obvious examples. Composers of operettas and musicals continued the trend with works such as Gilbert and Sullivan's *The Mikado* (1885, Japan) and Rodgers and Hammerstein's *The King and I* (1951, Thailand). Although these settings would have raised few eyebrows when the operas in question were written, the concept of 'exoticism' in opera is one that has been much discussed and frequently critiqued by scholars in recent years.

The nineteenth century was the heyday of Western imperialism. Britain ruled half the globe; France had substantial colonies in North Africa and the Middle East; and although neither Italy nor Germany possessed much in the way of an Empire, they certainly aspired to. This increasing contact with other cultures resulted in a growing fascination with the 'exotic' among artists of all kinds: painters, writers, and musicians. But their depictions of what they called the 'Orient' were not necessarily realistic: instead they created an imaginary Orient on to which Western audiences could project the products of their own imaginations. In other words, the East was effectively 'appropriated' for Western entertainment. Eastern peoples were often depicted as primitive and violent – the opposite of the supposed civilized West – yet submissive. The East was often depicted as representing freedom, licence, and pleasure – a place of loose morals and available nubile women. In the nineteenth century it was highly controversial to create an artistic representation of a naked woman from your own culture: the Impressionist painter Édouard Manet got into enormous trouble with his painting *Le Déjeuner sur l'herbe*, which depicted a nude woman picnicking with a group of fully clothed male friends. However, nudity was perfectly acceptable if the figure being painted (or sculpted) was distant from the spectator and the artist in some way, whether historically or geographically. So, an artist could get away with painting nudes if they were figures from antiquity or women supposedly from faraway parts of the globe. (I use the word 'supposedly' because many of the women in nineteenth-century paintings of harems and slave markets have fair hair and skin that denote them to be European.) Depicting images from the East almost became a sort of sanitized pornography.

Most nineteenth-century audience members were doubtless untroubled by the depictions of the 'Orient' that they saw around them. Their knowledge of non-Western cultures would, for the most part, have been fairly limited, leaving them in a poor position to judge the authenticity or otherwise of what was being depicted on stage (or displayed in an art gallery). However, it seems likely that many would have assumed that these art-works were providing them with a genuine 'window' onto the culture in question; some viewers may still do so today. Above all, most audience members would have regarded an Eastern-themed opera, say, as pure entertainment, the distant location merely enhancing the 'theatricality' of the work. It is improbable that any would have picked up on an imperialist subtext to the work; had they done so, they would have been extremely unlikely to have been offended by it, given how acceptable the concept of imperialism was to the vast majority of Westerners during the nineteenth century.

However, the depiction of non-Western cultures during this period is now regarded as discomfiting. 'Orientalism' has become a word with pejorative overtones, used to suggest simplistic and prejudiced portrayals of Eastern cultures by Western artists. The Palestinian writer Edward Said, a leading figure in post-colonial debates, has been particularly vocal in criticizing Orientalist artworks from the past in his books *Orientalism* and *Culture and Imperialism*. In the latter, he takes a number of canonical Western works, including Jane Austen's *Mansfield Park*, Conrad's *Heart of Darkness*, and, most significantly for our purposes, Verdi's *Aida*, and argues that they were shaped by an imperialist mentality and offered a justification for empire building. We might see *Aida*, in a way, as the ultimate exoticist fantasy, with its priests, slave girls, pyramids, grand triumphal arch, and (in many productions) camels, elephants, and so on. Nineteenth-century composers such as Verdi would have been likely to contend that their interest in Eastern settings was motivated by nothing more than a desire for colourful costumes and sets. But Said would argue that composers' motivations for choosing such subjects were more ideologically complex and that it is problematic, nowadays, to see these operas as innocent entertainment.

The composers of Orientalist operas have been criticized in particular because they tended to portray a stereotyped image of the East, both dramatically and musically, which paid little attention, in most cases, to the specific traits of the locale being depicted. Composers tended to rely upon a number of clichéd musical motifs that suggested a generalized 'Eastern' sound, whether the opera in question were set in China or (as McClary has shown) Spain. These included using notes and chords drawn from the chromatic scale (which uses all the white and black notes on a piano keyboard) or from the pentatonic scale (which uses only the black notes on a piano keyboard), unusual repeating rhythmic patterns, or unfamiliar-sounding percussion instruments.

Dramatically, operas set in Eastern locales tended to play into all the contemporary clichés about Eastern societies being despotic, cruel, licentious, and so on. One particular dramatic motif was especially prominent. According to Ralph Locke, the archetypal Orientalist opera plot goes as follows: 'a Western male becomes romantically involved with a local female, who is portrayed as sexually inviting and thereby at once attractive and threatening'. Thus, Eastern women were often depicted as seducing Western men against their will or better intentions (offering a twist on the familiar nineteenth-century *femme fatale* motif), ultimately leading them to their downfall – although in most cases it is the heroine who dies.

In Puccini's *Madama Butterfly* (1904) we have a sort of reversal of this clichéd scenario. The fifteen-year-old Ciò-Cio-San (or Butterfly) who is 'bought' by the US naval officer Pinkerton could hardly be said to have 'corrupted' her Western lover. Instead he purchases her as a straightforward financial transaction, with a lease on the marriage that is just as open to cancellation as the lease on the house he has taken on. The consequences of this thoughtless transaction will be profound and appalling for Cio-Cio San. She takes her new 'American' identity extremely seriously, breaking links with her own culture in the process. When Pinkerton goes back to America, she waits faithfully for his return, refusing to believe that her 'husband' has abandoned her. Ultimately, Pinkerton does return, but he has a 'real', American wife in tow, and the pair have come to collect the child Butterfly has borne and take him back to the United States to be raised as an American. In despair, Butterfly takes what she sees as the only honourable course of action and commits suicide.

This opera potentially raises many interesting debates about both gender and imperialism. In terms of gender politics, one might argue that this is a prime example of a male composer deliberately treating a female character in a 'sadistic' manner. Some have claimed that Puccini is particularly guilty of this offence: some of his heroines arguably suffer without any particular justification other than to give the audience a feeling of catharsis or to create a sense of closure to the opera. His über-sentimental operas leave some critics feeling rather queasy: they might argue that he and his librettists pluck at our heart-strings and prick our tear ducts to such an extent in this opera that it all becomes rather gratuitous. Butterfly's experience is certainly extremely painful to watch: the action moves so slowly in the second half of the opera that the audience feels as if it is sharing Butterfly's agonizing wait with her. But is Puccini deliberately being cruel to his heroine or merely empathizing with her? We might argue that Butterfly is the most positively depicted character in the opera: not a victim, but a naïve child who develops (both dramatically and musically) into a mature woman across the course of the opera. The male characters, on the other hand, are weak, cowardly, and distinctly unheroic.

Let's turn now to considering Puccini's depiction of Japan in this opera. The Eastern setting of *Madama Butterfly* seems less incidental than in many Orientalist works – Puccini and his librettists appear consciously more knowing about the implications of setting an opera in the East. This is not an opera that simply happens to take place in the Far East; rather, it consciously stages a confrontation between Eastern and Western cultures and seems to urge the listener to reflect upon the implications of one culture casually meddling in another's business. In part this is a somewhat less 'generic' portrayal of the East because the libretto was based upon a true story. Puccini's librettists Giuseppe Giacosa and Luigi Illica had based it upon a play by the American playwright David Belasco. This had itself been derived from a short story by an American writer called John Luther Long, which had in turn been based upon a true story recounted to Long by his sister, Jennie Correll, the wife of a missionary stationed in Nagasaki. As Arthur Groos has shown, the events recounted in the various Butterfly narratives took place in the early 1890s and were pretty close to the story of Puccini's opera, although the real-life geisha did not commit suicide, nor did the real-life sailor come back to collect his son.

Puccini was a composer who always researched the locales (and their sound worlds) for his operas scrupulously – for example, the precise pitch of the bells of the various churches in Rome in order to recreate the sound accurately in his opera *Tosca*. In preparing *Madama Butterfly* he did not have an opportunity to visit Japan but listened to early recordings of Japanese folk music and integrated some genuine Japanese themes into his score. He had a meeting with the wife of the Japanese ambassador to Italy in order to discuss Japanese customs and attended performances by the 'Imperial Japanese Theatrical Company' (led by the celebrated actress Sadayakko) on its tour of Italy in 1902. However, the fact that Puccini thought he was being more conscientious than many of his nineteenth-century predecessors in researching the music of the society he was depicting in no sense makes *Madama Butterfly* an 'authentic' Japanese work.

Puccini's audience would in any case have been none the wiser about whether the opera was 'authentic' or not, as their own knowledge of Japanese culture was extremely limited. There was a vogue for all things Japanese at this time – Japanese decorative *objets d'art* such as lacquered boxes, fans, and screens – and Western artists (including the Impressionists in France and the Macchiaioli movement in Italy) had consciously adapted Japanese motifs into their works and adapted Japanese techniques. But this was as far as most Westerners' knowledge of Japanese culture went. This limited knowledge was satirized by W. S. Gilbert, whose Japanese gentlemen in the chorus of *The Mikado* sing: 'If you want to know who we are, we are gentlemen of Japan; on many a vase and jar, on many a screen and fan'. Certainly, Puccini and his librettists played into all the clichés of Japanese people as small and decorative. In the Act One love duet, Butterfly sings: 'We are people accustomed to small things, humble and silent'. Meanwhile, a few years after composing the opera, Puccini admitted that he had been attracted to this character on account of the fact that she was 'a dear little woman, fragile and beloved like a Japanese doll, without pretensions'. Some scholars have argued that Puccini uses Butterfly as an emblem of Japan itself, reflecting a late nineteenth-century construction of Far Eastern cultures as weak and infantilized.

As noted in the previous chapter, Puccini has often been portrayed as an 'apolitical' composer. In Anthony Arblaster's book *Viva la libertà! Politics in Opera*, for example, the chapter on Puccini and Strauss is entitled 'Interlude – Opera Without Politics'. Helen Greenwald, meanwhile, has written that 'Puccini was more likely to equate power with sex than to explore a political issue. In general, Puccini considered politics an accessory'. However, the *Butterfly* narrative is an inescapably political one. Puccini's opera seems to offer us a set of important questions for which he and his librettists provide few clear answers. For example, we might ask whether *Madama Butterfly* is an imperialist or anti-imperialist work. The story certainly seems to depict an imperialist situation: the way in which Pinkerton treats Butterfly as a commodity to be bought and discarded at will seems to act as an allegory for Western colonialism and the plunder of other nations. However, from this might emerge another set of questions that are more difficult to answer. Was Puccini endorsing or condemning this situation (and does the composer's opinion matter either way)? Some commentators have become so overwhelmed by post-colonial guilt that they can no longer tolerate Puccini's opera, its music thoroughly tainted, in their view, by the grubbiness of its subject matter. Brian McIlroy (in a chapter in *A Vision of the Orient*) verges on suggesting censorship, demanding 'How can we endorse and endure the many *Madama Butterfly* narratives, given their origin in sexist, racist and imperialist notions of the East?' Likewise, in the same volume, Susan McClary writes 'I look forward to the day when we can pin this opera up in the museum of strange cultural practices of the past, when we can mount Puccini's *Butterfly* once and for all as a historical exhibit'.

However, these arguments hinge upon the assumption that Puccini and his librettists were complicit with the colonialist project. Whether you accept this point of view or not depends upon whether you see Puccini's sympathies as lying with Pinkerton or Butterfly. This is a difficult question to answer – as noted earlier, there has been much discussion in the Humanities recently of the dangers of relying upon 'authorial intention' in interpreting art-works. In a very simplistic way, we might point to the fact that there was something of the Pinkerton in Puccini – an inveterate womanizer – himself, although then we run into the veritable minefield of drawing simplistic connections between art and life. However, Pinkerton could certainly be seen as 'triumphing' at the end – he walks away from the situation, his conscience barely pricked (the original version of the opera did not even include Pinkerton's final remorseful aria, 'Addio fiorito asil'), with a 'proper' wife and his son. Equally, however, we might argue that Pinkerton comes across in the opera as a thoroughly weak and cowardly character and that so much of the opera is dedicated to exploring the psyche of Butterfly that our sympathies cannot but lie squarely with her at the end. Could *Madama Butterfly* be read, then, as an indictment of colonialism? Or, rather more depressingly, did Puccini just see an opportunity for a good old operatic tear-jerker? In other words, was he as guilty as the next colonialist of exploiting the East for his own financial gain? Was Japan just another picturesque setting for him, like Bohemian Paris in *La bohème*, or Gold Rush California in *La fanciulla del West*?

We might be tempted to draw parallels between *Madama Butterfly* and more recent clashes between the USA and Eastern cultures (the recent war in Iraq, for instance), and to argue that it is yet another example of 'American imperialism'. But to do so would be historically inaccurate and misleading: at the time when the opera was written, America by and large favoured a policy of political 'splendid isolation' (although it had certain economic interests in the East) and it was in fact Europeans who were guilty of the wholesale colonial plunder of Eastern countries. Nevertheless, the subject of *Madama Butterfly* remains powerful and topical today. The issue of Western control or a sense of superiority over non-Western countries is still a politically contentious one. The story of *Madama Butterfly* lends itself easily to updating, such as in the reworking of the opera as the musical *Miss Saigon*, in which the action is transferred to the Vietnam War.

Overall, the issue of Orientalism or exoticism in opera is a highly contentious one. One might argue, as Said and others have done, that these works are difficult to watch today because they are the product of an imperialist mentality – one might go as far as McClary and McIlroy and denounce them as racist, and even call for them to be banned. On the other hand, we might contend that these operas are a product of their time and that it would be wrong to transplant our twenty-first-century views onto art-works of the nineteenth century. Although it seems unfortunate, embarrassing, or even despicable now, imperialist views were commonplace among Europeans back in the nineteenth century, and composers were doing nothing exceptional in including these themes in their works. But in some cases, these operas can be read as a cautionary warning against imperialism, and perhaps this is the best way to read them today.

Epilogue

As I hope this book has shown, opera is a truly unique art-form – in fact, we might call it the ultimate multi-media form of art, bringing together as it does music, words, movement, acting, and design. It is this multi-disciplinary character that gives opera its vitality, although, as we saw in the introduction, opera's detractors have sometimes used this as evidence that opera is an 'impure' art-form, inferior to either straight drama or absolute music. Opera is also often perceived to be the most excessive of art-forms, characterized by grand passions, sumptuous costumes, lavish sets, and divas behaving badly both onstage and off. Yet despite this apparent separation from everyday life, operas (as we have seen) address the most fundamental and universal of human concerns – love, death, jealousy, greed, and power. However, it is sometimes seen as an art-form that belongs to earlier centuries. What is the place of opera in today's society?

Nowadays we often hear gloomy predictions from journalists and other commentators about the imminent death of classical music, opera included. It is true that opera faces a number of challenges today. It is difficult to get away from the fact that many operas (particularly from the core nineteenth-century repertory) are large in scale and highly costly to stage. As we have seen, operas are a collaborative effort both to create and to produce, involving a huge array of behind-the-scenes personnel (director, choreographer, set and costume designers, wig makers, stage hands, etc.) in addition to the performers and a large chorus and orchestra, plus a conductor and soloists who may charge large fees. Scenery and costumes are expensive, particularly for traditional stagings, and opera houses are often enormous institutions that cost a great deal to run. Of course, the business of staging operas was expensive in the past too, but it has become more so since the decline of aristocratic patronage. Throughout the twentieth century and into the twenty-first there have been frequent and heated debates about how the costs of staging opera should be covered. It is usually difficult to raise the necessary revenue from tickets alone (even if high prices are charged) and therefore government subsidies are sometimes granted to opera houses – the generosity of which varies from country to country, and which sometimes prompt political controversy.

Despite the economic challenges opera companies face today, the opera industry survives booms and busts with a hardiness that cannot fail to surprise cynical onlookers. There is still plainly an audience for operatic spectacle; indeed, productions at the world's most prestigious opera houses featuring celebrated singers often sell out within days or even hours. It would also be incorrect to surmise, as is sometimes suggested, that opera is something that appeals exclusively to older audiences. The most prestigious conservatoires across Europe and North America are inundated with applications from would-be opera singers, while a range of outreach projects and heavily discounted tickets have introduced new generations of listeners to opera. Indeed, one might argue that from the point of view of drawing in audiences the future looks much brighter for opera companies than it does for many symphony orchestras.

Opera's ongoing popularity can be attributed at least in some part to the fact that it successfully crosses boundaries between art and entertainment in ways that some other forms of classical music arguably do not. Opera today interacts with popular culture in a variety of ways that would seem to defy any claim of its belonging exclusively to a world of 'high art'. These include the widespread use of operatic extracts in film and advertising and the marketing of attractive young classical musicians in much the same way as pop stars. There is also the separate phenomenon of 'cross-over', in which professional opera singers such as Kiri Te Kanawa and Bryn Terfel record numbers from musicals, and 'celebrity singers' (such as Katherine Jenkins, a Welsh former school teacher) perform operatic arias. A number of recent television series have given 'ordinary people' a chance to take part in opera, such as the British series *Operatunity* (2003) – a cross between a talent contest and a fly-on-the-wall docu-soap, which sought to discover a singer with no professional training or experience who could be trained as an opera singer and put on stage at English National Opera (ENO) within a year. (A similar series in Australia, *Opera Oz*, followed in 2006.) Finally, opera has, in recent years, become associated with an unequivocally popular form of entertainment – football – since Luciano Pavarotti performed Puccini's 'Nessun Dorma' at the World Cup in Italy in 1990.

These developments have been seen as both positive and negative. The knee-jerk reaction of the purists is that these attempts to bring opera 'closer to the people' are nothing more than gimmicks, an example of opera being 'dumbed down'. Some scholars have put forward more reasoned arguments about the potential problems of reconciling classical music with popular culture, pointing out that art and popular culture have different norms and operate in fundamentally different ways. Julian Johnson, for instance, has attacked the commercially driven treatment of classical music as pop in his book *Who Needs Classical Music?* on the grounds that 'for all the appearance of difference, musics that derive from quite different functions lose their distinctiveness because they are assumed to serve the same functions as all the others'. He distinguishes classical music from other types of music on the grounds that it is 'discursive' music, which lends itself poorly to being heard in short chunks, or even played as background music. Generally speaking, Johnson proposes, classical music and popular music ideally require different types of listening; Lawrence Kramer likewise, in *Why Classical Music Still Matters*, argues that classical music 'wants to be explored, not just heard'.

Yet this argument about classical music demanding a particularly attentive type of listening is complicated in the case of opera – operas have always been 'fragmented' and commodified: think of eighteenth-century singers transporting arias from opera to opera, or nineteenth-century arias being sold in the form of sheet music for the public to sing at home or played in the street by barrel-organ grinders. Historically speaking, then, operatic music was often the object of distracted listening, just like popular music today. Furthermore, there have been times in opera's history when it has been regarded more as entertainment than as art. In later nineteenth-century Britain, for instance, opera was enjoyed by all strata of society. The working classes had many opportunities to encounter operatic music – through brass band arrangements, excerpts performed in music halls, and performances of complete operas throughout Britain by touring opera groups. Workers as well as employers up and down the country, and particularly in the industrial towns of the north, were able to enjoy a diverse range of operas, performed in English. The familiarity and popularity of operas by composers such as Verdi amongst the working classes is demonstrated by the fact that these works were gently satirized in popular burlesques. Likewise, opera was highly popular in the USA during the nineteenth century, its appeal cutting across all social classes: George Martin's book *Verdi at the Golden Gate*, for example, documents a thriving operatic culture in nineteenth-century San Francisco.

In the early twentieth century, opera in both the USA and the UK was increasingly segregated from other forms of entertainment, performed less frequently in English, and constructed as a 'higher' form of art that demanded hard work and was associated with a notion of taste and refinement seen to be the exclusive preserve of a certain social class. Opera acquired an image as a 'highbrow' art-form. Today, however, despite the clichés perpetuated in the media about opera being an exclusive or elitist art-form, we are seeing a return to ways in which opera was consumed by popular audiences prior to the twentieth century. Opera seems to be regaining something of its old 'entertainment' status, and for many people this is very much something to be welcomed. Even in our contemporary culture of sound bites and instant gratification, opera has the power to captivate audiences. Kramer emphasizes classical music's relationship to 'indispensable human concerns, the stuff of real life', arguing that certain types of classical music can offer us 'insight, intuition, and empathy'. As I hope this book has shown, opera can be exhilarating, exciting, comforting, cathartic, and much more. It is, I would argue, the branch of classical music that engages most directly with love, loss, sex, death, cruelty, kindness, jealousy, power, identity, community, and conflict: 'the stuff of real life' indeed.

Further reading

Chapter 1

Gallo, Denise: *Opera: The Basics* (New York: Routledge, 2006)

Groos, Arthur and Parker, Roger (eds): *Reading Opera* (Princeton, NJ: Princeton University Press, 1988)

Grout, Donald J. and Weigel Williams, Hermine: *A Short History of Opera* (New York: Columbia University Press, 4th edn, 2003)

Kerman, Joseph: *Opera as Drama* (London: Faber and Faber, 1989)

Parker, Roger (ed.): *The Oxford History of Opera* (Oxford: Oxford University Press, 1996)

Snowman, Daniel: *The Gilded Stage: A Social History of Opera* (London: Atlantic Books, 2009)

Weiss, Piero: *Opera: A History in Documents* (New York: Oxford University Press, 2002)

Chapter 2

Citron, Marcia: *Opera on Screen* (New Haven: Yale University Press, 2000)

Grover-Friedlander, Michal: *Vocal Apparitions: The Attraction of Cinema to Opera* (Princeton, NJ: Princeton University Press, 2005)

Joe, Jeongwon and Theresa, Rose (eds): *Between Opera and Cinema* (New York: Routledge, 2002)

Latham, Alison and Parker, Roger (eds): *Verdi in Performance* (Oxford: Oxford University Press, 2001)

Levin David J.: *Unsettling Opera: Staging Mozart, Verdi, Wagner, and Zemlinsky* (Chicago, IL: University of Chicago Press, 2007)

Radice, Mark A. (ed.): *Opera in Context: Essays on Historical Staging from the Late Renaissance to the Time of Puccini* (Portland, OR: Amadeus

Press, 1998) – see in particular the chapters by Evan Baker on Wagner and Verdi

Rutherford, Susan: *The Prima Donna and Opera, 1815–1930* (Cambridge: Cambridge University Press, 2006)

Wlaschin, Ken: *Encyclopedia of Opera on Screen: A Guide to More Than 100 Years of Opera Films, Videos, and DVDs* (New Haven: Yale University Press, 2004)

Chapter 3

Arblaster, Anthony: *Viva la libertà!: Politics in Opera* (London: Verso, 1992)

Bokina, John: *Opera and Politics: From Monteverdi to Henze* (New Haven, CT: Yale University Press, 1997)

Parker, Roger: *'Arpa d'or dei fatidici vati': The Verdian Patriotic Chorus in the 1840s* (Parma: Istituto nazionale di studi verdiani, 1997)

Smart, Mary-Ann: 'Verdi, Italian Romanticism, and the Risorgimento', in Scott: L. Balthazar (ed.): *The Cambridge Companion to Verdi* (Cambridge: Cambridge University Press, 2004)

Weiner, Marc A.: *Richard Wagner and the Anti-Semitic Imagination* (Lincoln: University of Nebraska Press, 1997)

Wilson, Alexandra: *The Puccini Problem: Opera, Nationalism, and Modernity* (Cambridge: Cambridge University Press, 2007/2009)

Chapter 4

Citron, Marcia: *Gender and the Musical Canon* (Urbana: University of Illinois Press, 2000)

Clément, Catherine: *Opera, or the Undoing of Woman* (London: Virago, 1989)

Locke, Ralph: *Musical Exoticism: Images and Reflections* (Cambridge: Cambridge University Press, 2009)

Said, Edward: *Orientalism* (Harmondsworth: Penguin, 1985)

—— *Culture and Imperialism* (London: Vintage, 1994)

Smart, Mary-Ann (ed.): *Siren Songs: Representations of Gender and*

Sexuality in Opera (Princeton, NJ: Princeton University Press, 2000)

Wisenthal, Jonathan, Grace, Sherrill, Boyd, Melinda, *et al.* (eds): *A Vision of the Orient: Texts, Intertexts, and Contexts of Madame Butterfly* (Toronto: University of Toronto Press, 2006)

Epilogue

Collins, Jim (ed.): *High-Pop: Making Culture into Popular Entertainment* (Oxford: Blackwell, 2002)

Johnson, Julian: *Who Needs Classical Music? Cultural Choice and Musical Value* (New York: Oxford University Press, 2002)

Kramer, Lawrence: *Why Classical Music Still Matters* (Berkeley: University of California Press, 2007)

Levine, Lawrence W.: Highbrow/Lowbrow: The Emergence of Cultural Hierarchy in America (Cambridge, MA: Harvard University Press, 1988)

Payne, Nicholas: 'Opera in the Marketplace', in Cooke (ed.), *The Cambridge Companion to Twentieth-Century Opera* (Cambridge: Cambridge University Press, 2005)

Wilson, Alexandra: 'Killing Time: Contemporary Representations of Opera in British Culture', *Cambridge Opera Journal* 19/3 (November 2007), 249–70

Bibliography

Abbate, Carolyn: *In Search of Opera* (Princeton, NJ: Princeton University Press, 2001)

Balthazar, Scott L. (ed.): *The Cambridge Companion to Verdi* (Cambridge: Cambridge University Press, 2004)

Basini, Laura: 'Cults of Sacred Memory: Parma and the Verdi Centennial Celebrations of 1913', *Cambridge Opera Journal* 13/2 (July 2001), 141–61

Bellman, Jonathan (ed.): *The Exotic in Western Music* (Boston, MA: Northeastern University Press, 1998)

Benjamin, Walter: 'The Work of Art in the Age of Mechanical Reproduction', in Hannah Arendt (ed.), *Illuminations* (London: Fontana Press, 1992)

Bianconi, Lorenzo and Walker, Thomas: 'Production, Consumption, and Political Function of Seventeenth-Century Opera', *Early Music History* 4 (1984), 209–96

Blackmer, Corinne E. and Smith, Patricia Juliana (eds.): *En Travesti: Women, Gender Subversion, Opera* (New York: Columbia University Press, 1995)

Brown-Montesano, Kristi: *Understanding the Women of Mozart's Operas* (Berkeley: University of California Press, 2007)

Budden, Julian: *Puccini: His Life and Works* (Oxford: Oxford University Press, 2002)

—— *Verdi* (New York: Oxford University Press, 3rd edn, 2008)

Busch, Hans: *Verdi's* Aida: *The History of an Opera in Letters and Documents* (Minneapolis: University of Minnesota Press, 1982) – contains a disposizione scenica in translation, as does the item below

—— (ed.): *Verdi's* Otello *and* Simon Boccanegra *(Revised Version) in Letters and Documents* (Oxford: Clarendon Press, 1988)

Carner, Mosco: *Puccini: A Critical Biography* (London: Duckworth, 3rd edn, 1992)

Charlton, David (ed.): *The Cambridge Companion to Grand Opera* (Cambridge: Cambridge University Press, 2005)

Chusid, Martin: 'On Censored Performances of *Les Vêpres siciliennes* and *Rigoletto*: Evidence from the Verdi Archive at New York University', *The Verdi Newsletter*, 25 (1998)

Cooke, Mervyn (ed.): *The Cambridge Companion to Benjamin Britten* (Cambridge: Cambridge University Press, 1999)

Cooke, Mervyn (ed.): *The Cambridge Companion to Twentieth-Century Opera* (Cambridge: Cambridge University Press, 2005)

Cowen, Tyler: *In Praise of Commercial Culture* (Cambridge, MA: Harvard University Press, 1998)

Dahlhaus, Carl: 'What is a Musical Drama?', *Cambridge Opera Journal*, 1/2 (July 1989), 95–111

Daverio, John: *Robert Schumann: Herald of a New Poetic Era* (New York: Oxford University Press, 1997)

Dellamora, Richard and Fischlin, Daniel (eds.): *The Work of Opera: Genre, Nationhood, and Sexual Difference* (New York, Columbia University Press, 1997)

Dijkstra, Bram: *Idols of Perversity: Fantasies of Feminine Evil in Fin-de-Siècle Culture* (Oxford: Oxford University Press, 1986)

DiMaggio, Paul: 'Cultural Boundaries and Structural Change: The Extension of the High Culture Model to Theater, Opera, and the Dance, 1900–1940', in Michèle Lamont and Marcel Fournier (eds), *Cultivating Differences: Symbolic Boundaries and the Making of Inequality* (Chicago, IL: University of Chicago Press, 1992)

Feldman, Martha: *Opera and Sovereignty: Transforming Myths in Eighteenth-Century Italy* (Chicago, IL: University of Chicago Press, 2007)

Forsyth, Cecil: *Music and Nationalism: A Study of English Opera* (London: Macmillan, 1911)

Giger, Andreas: 'Social Control and the Censorship of Giuseppe

Verdi's Operas in Rome (1844–1859)', *Cambridge Opera Journal* 11/3 (November 1999), 233–66

Gilbert, Shirli: *Music in the Holocaust: Confronting Life in the Nazi Ghettos and Camps* (Oxford: Clarendon Press, 2005)

Girardi, Michele: *Puccini: His International Art* (Chicago, IL: University of Chicago Press, 2003)

Gossett, Philip: 'Becoming a Citizen: The Chorus in *Risorgimento* Opera', *Cambridge Opera Journal* 2/1 (March 1990), 41–64

—— *Divas and Scholars: performing Italian Opera* (Chicago, IL: University of Chicago Press, 2006)

Greenwald, Helen: 'Verdi's Patriarch and Puccini's Matriarch: "Through the Looking-Glass and What Puccini Found There"', *Nineteenth-Century Music* 17/3 (Spring 1994), 220–36

Grey, Thomas S. (ed.): *The Cambridge Companion to Wagner* (Cambridge: Cambridge University Press, 2008)

Groos, Arthur: 'Madame Butterfly: The Story', *Cambridge Opera Journal* 3/2 (July 1991), 125–58

Hall-Witt, Jennifer: *Fashionable Acts: Opera and Elite Culture in London, 1780–1880* (Durham: University of New Hampshire Press, 2007)

Heartz, Daniel (ed.): *Mozart's Operas* (Berkeley: University of California Press, 1990)

Henson, Karen: 'Verdi, Victor Maurel and *Fin-de-Siècle* Operatic Performance', *Cambridge Opera Journal* 19/1 (March 2007), 59–84

Hibberd, Sarah: *French Grand Opera and the Historical Imagination* (Cambridge: Cambridge University Press, 2009)

Hudson, Elizabeth: 'Gilda Seduced: A Tale Untold', *Cambridge Opera Journal* 4/3 (November 1992), 229–51

Hunter, Mary: *The Culture of Opera Buffa in Mozart's Vienna: A Poetics of Entertainment* (Princeton, NJ: Princeton University Press, 1999)

—— *Mozart's Operas: A Companion* (New Haven: Yale University Press, 2008)

Hutcheon, Linda and Hutcheon, Michael: *Opera: Desire, Disease, Death* (Lincoln: University of Nebraska Press, 1996)

—— *Opera: The Art of Dying* (Cambridge, MA: Harvard University Press, 2004)

Johnson, Victoria, Fulcher, Jane F. and Ertman, Thomas (eds): *Opera and Society in Italy and France from Monteverdi to Bourdieu* (Cambridge: Cambridge University Press, 2007)

Kimbell, David: *Opera in the Age of Italian Romanticism* (Cambridge: Cambridge University Press, 1985)

—— *Italian Opera* (Cambridge: Cambridge University Press, 1991)

Kolb, Bonita M.: *Marketing for Cultural Organisations: New Strategies for Attracting Audiences to Classical Music, Dance, Museums, Theatre, and Opera* (London: Thomson Learning, 2nd edn., 2005)

Lacombe, Hervé: *The Keys to French Opera in the Nineteenth Century* (Berkeley: University of California Press, 2001)

Leech, Caroline: *Welsh National Opera – Celebrating the First Sixty Years* (Cardiff: Graffeg, 2006)

Lindenberger, Herbert: *Opera in History: From Monteverdi to Cage* (Stanford, CT: Stanford University Press, 1998)

Locke, Ralph: 'Constructing the Oriental "Other": Saint-Saëns's *Samson et Dalila*', *Cambridge Opera Journal* 3/3 (1991), 261–302

Magee, Bryan: *Wagner and Philosophy* (London: Penguin, 2001)

Martin, George: *Verdi at the Golden Gate: Opera and San Francisco in the Gold Rush Years* (Berkeley: University of California Press, 1993)

McClary, Susan: *Georges Bizet: Carmen* (Cambridge: Cambridge University Press, 1992)

Millington, Barry: *The New Grove Guide to Wagner and His Operas* (New York: Oxford University Press, 2006)

Montemorra Marvin, Roberta: 'The Censorship of Verdi's Operas in Victorian London', *Music and Letters*, 82/4 (November 2001), 582–610

—— 'Verdian opera burlesqued: a glimpse into mid-Victorian theatrical culture', *Cambridge Opera Journal* 15/1 (March 2003), 33–66

Parker, Roger: *Leonora's Last Act* (Princeton, NJ: Princeton University Press, 1997)

—— *The New Grove Guide to Verdi and His Operas* (New York: Oxford University Press, 2007)

—— *Remaking the Song: Operatic Visions and Revisions from Handel to Berio* (Berkeley: University of California Press, 2006)

Phillips-Matz, Mary-Jane: *Verdi: A Biography* (Oxford: Oxford University Press: 1993)

Prest, Julia: *Theatre Under Louis XIV: Cross Casting and the Performance of Gender in Drama, Ballet and Opera* (New York: Palgrave MacMillan, 2006)

Rosand, Ellen: *Opera in Seventeenth-Century Venice: The Creation of a Genre* (Berkeley: University of California Press, 2007)

—— *Monteverdi's Last Operas: A Venetian Trilogy* (Berkeley: University of California Press, 2007)

Rosselli, John: *The Life of Verdi* (Cambridge: Cambridge University Press, 2000)

—— *Music and Musicians in Nineteenth-Century Italy* (London: Batsford, 1991)

—— *Singers of Italian Opera: The History of a Profession* (Cambridge: Cambridge University Press, 1992)

Russell, David: *Popular Music in England, 1840–1914: A Social History* (Manchester: Manchester University Press, 2nd edn, 1997)

Rutherford, Susan: '"La cantante delle passioni": Giuditta Pasta and the Idea of Operatic Performance', *Cambridge Opera Journal* 19/2 (July 2007), 107–38

Schroeder, David: *Cinema's Illusions, Opera's Allure* (New York: Continuum, 2002)

Smart, Mary-Ann: *Mimomania: Music and Gesture in Nineteenth-Century Opera* (Berkeley: University of California Press, 2004)

Steptoe, Andrew: *The Mozart-Da Ponte Operas: The Cultural and Musical Background* (Oxford: Clarendon Press, 1988)

Storey, John: '"Expecting Rain": Opera as Popular Culture', in Jim Collins (ed.), *High-Pop: Making Culture into Popular Entertainment* (Oxford: Blackwell, 2002)

Sutcliffe, Tom: *Believing in Opera* (London: Faber and Faber, 1996)

Tambling, Jeremy: *Opera, Ideology and Film* (Manchester: Manchester University Press, 1987)

Tanner, Michael: *Wagner* (London: HarperCollins, 1997)

Taruskin, Richard: 'Music's Dangers and the Case for Control', *New York Times*, 9 December 2001

Tusa, Michael C.: 'Beethoven's Essay in Opera: Historical, Text-Critical, and Interpretative Issues in *Fidelio*', in Glenn Stanley (ed.), *The Cambridge Companion to Beethoven* (Cambridge: Cambridge University Press, 2000)

Tyrrell, John: *Czech Opera* (Cambridge: Cambridge University Press, 1988)

Vandiver Nicassio, Susan: *Tosca's Rome* (Chicago, IL: University of Chicago Press, 2002)

Wagner, Richard: *Judaism in Music*, trans. Edwin Evans (London: William Reeves, 1910)

Warrack, John: *German Opera: From the Beginnings to Wagner* (Cambridge: Cambridge University Press, 2001)

Weaver, William and Puccini, Simonetta: *The Puccini Companion* (Norton, 2000)

Wilson, Alexandra: 'Torrefranca vs Puccini: Embodying a Decadent Italy', *Cambridge Opera Journal* 13/1 (2001), 29–53

Zelechow, Bernard: 'The Opera: The Meeting of Popular and Elite Culture in the Nineteenth Century', *Journal of Popular Culture* 25/2 (1991), 91–7

Recommended listening/viewing

Below is a list of operas discussed in this book, some of which you may wish to listen to in conjunction with reading the text. Thereafter I have provided an additional list of operas that I would recommend for readers wishing to take their interest in opera further. For the reader who is completely new to opera, I would suggest that a 'starter collection' of recordings providing a broad overview of the art-form might include works by the following composers: Purcell, Handel, Mozart, Rossini, Verdi, Bizet, Wagner, Puccini, and Britten.

Operas discussed in the book

Seventeenth century:
    Monteverdi, *Orfeo*
    Monteverdi, *L'incoronazione di Poppea*
    Peri, *Euridice*
    Purcell, *Dido and Aeneas*
Eighteenth century:
    Gluck, *Alceste*
    Gluck, *Orfeo ed Euridice*
    Handel, *Rinaldo*
    Mozart, *La clemenza di Tito*
    Mozart, *Così fan tutte*
    Mozart, *Don Giovanni*
    Mozart, *Die Entführung aus dem Serail*
    Mozart, *Idomeneo*
    Mozart, *Le nozze di Figaro*

Mozart, *Die Zauberflöte*
Pergolesi, *La serva padrona*
Nineteenth century:
Auber, *La Muette de Portici*
Balfe, *The Bohemian Girl*
Beethoven, *Fidelio*
Bellini, *Norma*
Bizet, *Carmen*
Bizet, *Les Pêcheurs des perles*
Delibes, *Lakmé*
Donizetti, *Anna Bolena*
Donizetti, *Lucia di Lammermoor*
Donizetti, *Maria Stuarda*
Gilbert and Sullivan, *The Mikado*
Giordano, *La mala vita*
Glinka, *Ruslan and Lyudmila*
Gounod, *Faust*
Halévy, *La Juive*
Mascagni, *Cavalleria rusticana*
Mascagni, *Iris*
Massenet, *Thaïs*
Puccini, *La bohème*
Rossini, *Otello*
Sullivan, *Ivanhoe*
Tchaikovsky, *Eugene Onegin*
Verdi, *Aida*
Verdi, *Un ballo in maschera*
Verdi, *La battaglia di Legnano*
Verdi, *I due foscari*
Verdi, *Ernani*
Verdi, *Falstaff*
Verdi, *I Lombardi alla prima crociata*
Verdi, *Macbeth*
Verdi, *Nabucco*

Verdi, *Oberto*
Verdi, *Otello*
Verdi, *Rigoletto*
Verdi, *Simon Boccanegra*
Verdi, *Stiffelio*
Verdi, *La traviata*
Verdi, *Il trovatore*
Wagner, *Götterdämmerung*
Wagner, *Die Meistersinger von Nürnberg*
Wagner, *Parsifal*
Wagner, *Das Rheingold*
Wagner, *Siegfried*
Wagner, *Tristan und Isolde*
Wagner, *Die Walküre*
Weber, *Der Freischütz*
Twentieth century:
Adams, *The Death of Klinghoffer*
Adams, *Nixon in China*
Adès, *Powder her Face*
Barber, *Antony and Cleopatra*
Bartók, *Duke Bluebeard's Castle*
Berg, *Lulu*
Berg, *Wozzeck*
Bernstein, *Candide*
Britten, *Peter Grimes*
Charpentier, *Louise*
Cilea, *Adriana Lecouvreur*
Debussy, *Pelléas et Mélisande*
Gershwin, *Porgy and Bess*
Glass, *Satyagraha*
Korngold, *Die Tote Stadt*
Puccini, *La fanciulla del West*
Puccini, *Gianni Schicchi*
Puccini, *Madama Butterfly*

Puccini, *Il tabarro*
Puccini, *Tosca*
Puccini, *Turandot*
Schoenberg, *Erwartung*
Smyth, *The Wreckers*
Strauss, *Ariadne auf Naxos*
Strauss, *Elektra*
Strauss, *Salome*
Stravinsky, *Oedipus Rex*
Stravinsky, *The Rake's Progress*
Wallace, *The Bonesetter's Daughter*

Further listening

Seventeenth century:
Lully, *Armide*
Monteverdi, *Il ritorno d'Ulisse in patria*
Purcell, *The Fairy Queen*
Eighteenth century:
Gay, *The Beggar's Opera*
Handel, *Ariodante*
Handel, *Giulio Cesare*
Handel, *Tamerlano*
Rameau, *Hippolyte et Aricie*
Vivaldi, *Tito Manlio*
Nineteenth century:
Bellini, *I puritani*
Bellini, *La sonnambula*
Berlioz, *Benvenuto Cellini*
Berlioz, *Les Troyens*
Borodin, *Prince Igor*
Catalani, *La Wally*
Donizetti, *L'elisir d'amore*
Gounod, *Roméo et Juliette*

Massenet, *Manon*
Meyerbeer, *Les Huguenots*
Meyerbeer, *Robert le diable*
Mussorgsky, *Boris Godunov*
Offenbach, *Les Contes d'Hoffmann*
Offenbach, *Orphée aux enfers*
Ponchielli, *La Gioconda*
Puccini, *Manon Lescaut*
Rossini, *Il barbiere di Siviglia*
Rossini, *La Cenerentola*
Rossini, *Guillaume Tell*
Rossini, *L'italiana in Algeri*
Rossini, *Tancredi*
Saint-Saëns, *Samson et Dalila*
Smetana, *The Bartered Bride*
Spontini, *La vestale*
Thomas, *Hamlet*
Wagner, *Lohengrin*
Wagner, *Tannhäuser*
Twentieth century:
Birtwistle, *The Mask of Orpheus*
Britten, *Billy Budd*
Britten, *Death in Venice*
Britten, *The Turn of the Screw*
Dukas, *Ariane et Barbe-Bleue*
Dvořák, *Rusalka*
Janáček, *The Cunning Little Vixen*
Janáček, *Jenůfa*
Janáček, *Katya Kabanova*
Krenek, *Jonny spielt auf*
Leoncavallo, *I pagliacci*
Poulenc, *Les Dialogues des Carmelites*
Ravel, *L'Heure espagnole*
Schoenberg, *Moses und Aron*

Shostakovich, *Lady Macbeth of the Mtsensk District*
Strauss, *Der Rosenkavalier*
Tippett, *King Priam*
Tippett, *The Midsummer Marriage*

Index

Abbiati, Franco 87, 88
Adams, John 45, 94, 106
   Death of Klinghoffer 45, 94
   Nixon in China 45, 106
Adès, Thomas 44, 94, 106
   Powder her Face 94
Adriana Lecouvreur 110
Aida 25, 58, 63, 120, 122
Aix-en-Provence 57
Alceste 14
Alfano, Franco 38
Allen, Woody 75
alto 15
America 38, 44–5, 74, 124,
   128, 131; *see also* USA
Andromeda 5
Anna Bolena 22
anti-Semitism 100–6
Antony and Cleopatra 71
Appia, Adolphe 53
Arblaster, Anthony 126
aria 3, 6, 8, 12, 13, 14, 20, 21,
   26, 31, 37, 38, 49, 60,
   127, 132, 133
Ariadne auf Naxos 49
Athens 29
Auber, Daniel 24, 25, 110
   La Muette de Portici 24, 110
Austen, Jane 122
   Mansfield Park 122
Australia 71, 132
Austria 81, 83, 84, 85

'authentic' performance 55,
   58, 59, 60, 62, 67

Balfe, Michael 34
   The Bohemian Girl 34
ballet 8, 24, 56, 61, 111
Un ballo in maschera 64
Balzac, Honoré de 112
   *Splendeurs et misères des
   courtisanes* 112
Barber, Samuel 71
   Antony and Cleopatra 71
Barcelona 64
Barenboim, Daniel 105–6
baritone 15
Barthes, Roland 66
Bartók, Béla 42
   Duke Bluebeard's Castle 42
bass 15, 18, 103
La battaglia di Legnano 85
Bayreuth Festspielhaus 29, 30,
   52, 53
BBC (British Broadcasting
   Corporation) 71–2
BBC Concert Orchestra 72
Beaumarchais, Pierre-Augustin
   17, 22, 80, 81
Beethoven, Ludwig van ix, 32,
   105
   Fidelio 32
bel canto 22

Belasco, David 125
Bellini, Vincenzo 22
   Norma 22
Benjamin, Walter 77–8
   'The Work of Art in the
      Age of Mechanical
      Reproduction' 77
Berg, Alban 42
   Lulu 42
   Wozzeck 42
Bergman, Ingmar 75
Berlin 65
Bernstein, Leonard 44
   Candide 44
Bertoja, Giuseppe 53
Bieito, Calixto 64–5
Birmingham 69
Birtwistle, Harrison 44
Bizet, Georges 33, 36, 72, 105,
      120
   Carmen 33, 36, 110, 120
   Les Pêcheurs des perles 33,
      120
La bohème 46, 48, 49, 128
The Bohemian Girl 34
The Bonesetter's Daughter 48
Boughton, Rutland 43
Bourbon Dynasty 84
bourgeoisie 41, 112
Britain 9, 34, 43, 69, 109, 121,
      133; *see also* England
Britten, Benjamin 44
   Peter Grimes 44
Bronx 65
Brussels 58
burlesque 133
Byron, Lord 27
   The Two Foscari 27

cabaletta 21, 26
Caccini, Francesca 109
California 128
Callas, Maria 50, 75
Candide 44
canonicity 33, 45, 46, 70, 105,
      108, 109
cantabile 21
Carmen 33, 36, 110, 120
Caruso, Enrico 37, 73
Casella, Alfredo 39
castrato 8, 13–14, 61
Cavalleria rusticana 37
Cavalli, Francesco 7
censorship 28, 81–2, 85,
      89–95, 127
Ceylon (Sri Lanka) 33, 120
Chabrier, Emmanuel 33
chamber music 82, 108
chamber opera 35, 42, 46
Charpentier, Gustave 37
   Louise 37
Chausson, Ernest 33
China 120, 123
choral music 15, 26, 82
choreographer 55, 56, 130
chorus 4, 8, 23, 25, 56, 72,
      85–8, 91, 126, 130
chromaticism 40, 123
Cilea, Francesco 36, 110
   Adriana Lecouvreur 110
Citron, Marcia 75, 78
Classic FM 94
Clément, Catherine 114–17
La clemenza di Tito 15
coloratura 15
comic opera 15–19, 116
commedia dell'arte 16

concerto 82, 109
conductor 48, 88, 105, 130
Conrad, Joseph 122
    Heart of Darkness 122
Corbiau, Gérard 14
Cornwall 30
Correll, Jennie 125
Corsi, Jacopo 3
Così fan tutte 17
counter tenor 14
critical edition 59
Czech opera 34, 43

da capo aria 12, 13, 14, 21
Dafne 3
La Dame aux camélias 27,
    112–13
Da Ponte, Lorenzo 17, 18, 80,
    81
Death of Klinghoffer 45, 94
Debussy, Claude 38, 39, 41
    Pelléas et Mélisande 39–40, 41
Delibes, Léo 33, 120
    Lakmé 33, 120
Dido and Aeneas 8
director 48, 49, 52, 53, 54, 55,
    57, 58, 63, 64–6, 67,
    74–5, 76, 77, 78, 130
disposizione scenica, see staging
    manual
divertissement 8
Don Giovanni 17–19, 65
Donizetti, Gaetano 22, 120
    Anna Bolena 22
    Emilia di Liverpool 120
    Lucia di Lammermoor 22, 120
    Maria Stuarda 22
I due Foscari 27

duet 3, 6, 95, 126
Duke Bluebeard's Castle 42
Dumas, Alexandre 27, 112–13
    La Dame aux camélias 27,
    112–13
Dun, Tan 45
Duplessis, Marie 113
Dvořák, Antonin 34

Egypt 33, 120
Elektra 40
Emilia di Liverpool 120
England 8–9, 10, 34
English National Opera 63, 65,
    132
Enlightenment 20, 81
Die Entführung aus dem Serail
    65, 119
Ernani 27, 86, 92
Erwartung 41–2
Esterhaza court 82
Ethnomusicology 119
Eugene Onegin 34, 109
Euphrates, River 86
Euridice 3, 4, 109
exoticism 22, 33, 41, 119–23,
    128
Expressionism 41

Falstaff 26, 28
La fanciulla del West 128
Farinelli (Carlo Maria Broschi)
    13
Farinelli (film) 14
Fascism 98, 99
Faust 74
feminism 107–8, 114, 118, 119

Ferrari, Benedetto 5
  Andromeda 5
Fidelio 32
film 14, 36, 44, 47–8, 49, 63,
    74–8, 116, 131
finale 18–19
First World War 104
Flashmob the Opera 71–2
Florence 1, 2, 4, 38, 84, 91,
    109
Florentine Camerata 2, 3, 109
football 38, 72, 132
Forsyth, Cecil 43
France 4, 7–8, 21, 22, 23–4,
    33, 39–40, 43, 51, 60–1,
    70, 80, 81, 86, 91, 92, 97,
    110, 112, 121, 126
François I of France 93
Der Freischütz 23
French Revolution 17, 24, 81
Freud, Sigmund 41
Friedrich, Caspar David 22

Gandhi, Mahatma 106
Garnier, Charles 70
Gatti, Carlo 87
Gatti, Guido M. 95
Gaul 22
Germany 7, 14, 23, 28–30, 33,
    40, 43, 45, 97, 100, 101,
    102, 104–5, 109, 121
Gershwin, George 44
  Porgy and Bess 44
Giacosa, Giuseppe 125
Gianni Schicchi 75
Gilbert, Shirli 105
Gilbert, W. S. 9, 34, 120, 126;
    see also Sullivan, Arthur
Giordano, Umberto 36
  La mala vita 36
Giselle 111
Giza 76
Glass, Philip 45, 106
  Satyagraha 106
Glinka, Mikhail 34
  Ruslan and Lyudmila 34
Globe Theatre (London) 62
Gluck, Christoph Willibald
    14–15, 60–1
  Alceste 14
  Orfeo ed Euridice 60, 61
  Orphée et Eurydice 60
Gobbi, Tito 75
The Godfather 63
Goldoni, Carlo 17
Gonzaga, Duke Vincenzo of 4,
    5
Götterdämmerung 29
Gounod, Charles 74
  Faust 74
Gran Teatro la Fenice (Venice)
    53, 93
Gran Teatro del Liceu
    (Barcelona) 64
Grand Opera 23–4, 25, 28, 34,
    86, 110
Greece 34, 68
Greenwald, Helen 126
Groos, Arthur 125
ground bass 8

Habsburg monarchy 81
Halévy, Fromental 110
  La Juive 110

Hammerstein II, Oscar 120
Handel, George Frideric 9,
    10–11
  Rinaldo 11
Hanslick, Eduard 103
Hasse, Johann Adolph 16
Haussmann, Baron 70
haute contre 8, 61
Haydn, Joseph 82
Henri IV of France 3–4
Hitler, Adolf 104–5
Hoffmann, E. T. A. 23
  Undine 23
Holy Land 85
Hopper, Edward 63
  Nighthawks 63
Hugo, Victor 27, 91, 92, 93,
    120
  Hernani 27
  Les Orientales 120
  Le Roi s'amuse 27, 91
Hungary 34

Idomeneo 15
Illica, Luigi 125
imperialism 118–29
Impressionism 121, 126
L'incoronazione di Poppea 6
India 33, 120
D'Indy, Vincent 32, 33
intermedi 2
intermezzi 16
interval 18, 42
Iraq 79, 128
Ireland 34
Iris 110
Israel 105–6
Italy 1–7, 9–11, 15–16, 20–2,
    25–8, 33, 35–9, 43, 51,
    53, 68, 81, 82–100, 113,
    120, 121, 125, 126, 132
Ivanhoe 34

Janáček, Leoš 43
Japan 38, 120, 124, 125–6, 128
Jenkins, Katherine 132
Johnson, Julian 132
Jommelli, Niccolò 10
Joseph II of Austria 19, 81
La Juive 110

The King and I 120
Kingdom of Sardinia 84
Kingdom of the Two Sicilies
    84
Komische Oper (Berlin) 65
Korngold, Erich 48
  Die Tote Stadt 48
Kramer, Lawrence 133, 134

Lakmé 33, 120
Legnano 85
Leitmotiv 32, 33
Leo, Leonardo 10
Leoncavallo, Ruggero 36, 97
libretto 8, 10, 11, 20, 24, 36,
    40, 41, 48, 59, 80, 89, 90,
    92, 93, 94, 114, 125
Lincoln Center 70
Little Italy 63
Locke, Ralph 123
I Lombardi alla prima crociata 85
London 11, 40, 43, 44, 49, 62,
    65, 68, 71, 75

Long, John Luther 125
Los Angeles Opera 75
Louis XIV of France 8, 24
Louise 37
Lucia di Lammermoor 22, 120
Lully, Jean-Baptiste 7, 8, 80
Lulu 42

Macbeth 27, 28, 61, 86, 91
Macchiaioli movement 126
Madama Butterfly 113–14, 120,
    123–8
Maeterlinck, Maurice 39
    Pelléas et Mélisande 39
mafia 63, 64
Magee, Bryan 104
The Magic Flute 19, 20, 75
La mala vita 36
Malipiero, Gian Francesco 39
Manelli, Francesco 5
Manet, Édouard 121
Mantua 4, 5
Maria Stuarda 22
Marie Antoinette, Queen of
    France 81
The Marriage of Figaro 17, 22,
    46, 80–1, 116, 118
Martin, George 133
Mascagni, Pietro 36, 37, 96,
    110
    Cavalleria rusticana 37
    Iris 110
masque 8
Massenet, Jules 33
    Thaïs 33
Mazzini, Giuseppe 84, 85
McClary, Susan 107, 120, 123,
    127, 128

McIlroy, Brian 127, 128
McVicar, David 64
Medici family 2, 109
Medici, Maria de 3
Die Meistersinger von Nürnberg
    29, 103–4
Melba, Nellie 49
Mendelssohn, Felix 101, 102
Metastasio, Pietro 10
Metropolitan Opera (New
    York) 48, 70, 74
Meyerbeer, Giacomo 25, 101
mezzo-soprano 15
The Mikado 120, 126
Milan 21, 83, 85, 88, 91
Millais, John Everett 111
Miller, Jonathan 63–4
Miss Saigon 128
Mitterrand, François 70
Modena 95
modernism 39, 41, 42
Molière (Jean-Baptiste
    Poquelin) 17
Molina, Tirso de 17
Monaldi, Gino 87
monody 2
Monteverdi, Claudio 4–5, 6,
    109
    L'incoronazione di Poppea 6
    Orfeo 4, 6
Montmartre 37
Moreschi, Alessandro 14
motif 23, 32, 41, 123, 126
Mount Vesuvius 24, 110
Mozart, Wolfgang Amadeus 15,
    16–20, 22, 65, 72, 80–1,
    82, 105, 118, 119–20
    La clemenza di Tito 15
    Così fan tutte 17

Mozart (*cont.*):
  Don Giovanni 17–19, 65
  Die Entführung aus dem Serail
    65, 119
  Idomeneo 15
  The Magic Flute 19, 20, 75
  The Marriage of Figaro 17, 22,
    46, 80–1, 116, 118
  *Le nozze di Figaro, see The
    Marriage of Figaro*
  *Die Zauberflöte, see The Magic
    Flute*
La Muette de Portici 24, 110
musical 20, 44, 120
music drama 29
Mussorgsky, Modest 34

Nabucco 27, 86–8
Nagasaki 125
Naples 15, 24, 89, 90, 91
National Singspiel 20
Nazism 45, 100, 102, 104–5
Nebuchadnezzar, King 86
neoclassicism 42
New Testament 40, 91
New York 48, 57, 63, 65, 70,
  74
Nielsen, Carl 43
Nixon in China 45, 106
Noh theatre 58
Norma 22
*Le nozze di Figaro, see The
  Marriage of Figaro*
Nuremberg 103

Oberto: conte di San Bonifacio 26
Oedipus Rex 42
Old Testament 86

one-act opera 37, 40, 42
Opéra de la Bastille (Paris) 70
opera buffa 15–18, 82
Opéra Garnier (Paris) 70
Opera Oz 132
opera seria 10, 14–15, 16, 22,
  80, 82
Operatunity 132
operetta 9, 34, 120
oratorio 43, 109
orchestra 3, 6, 9, 22, 23, 24,
  30, 31, 32, 33, 35, 40, 41,
  42, 52, 61, 72, 77, 105,
  130, 131
Orfeo (Monteverdi) 4, 6
Orfeo ed Euridice (Gluck) 60–1
Orientalism 33, 122–3, 124–5,
  128
Orphée et Eurydice (Gluck)
  60–1
ornamentation 12, 22, 60
Otello (Rossini) 28
Otello (Verdi) 27, 28, 57
Ottoman Empire 119
overture 8, 9

Paddington Station (London)
  71–2
Paisiello, Giovanni 16
Palermo 91
Palestine 94, 120, 122
pantomime 16
Paris 7, 21, 23, 37, 60, 70, 80,
  81, 128
Parker, Roger 87–8
Parma 25, 83
Parsifal 29, 52, 104
Parthenon, the 69

pasticcio 6
patronage 2, 4, 13, 31, 35, 45, 69, 79, 81, 82, 131
Pavarotti, Luciano 132
Les Pêcheurs des perles 33, 120
Pelléas et Mélisande 39–40, 41
Pergolesi, Giovanni Battista 16
  La serva padrona 16
Peri, Jacopo 3, 4, 109
  Dafne 3
  Euridice 3, 4, 109
Peter Grimes 44
Piave, Francesco Maria 92, 93
Piedmont 83, 89
Pissaro, Camille 102
Pizzetti, Ildebrando 39
Poe, Edgar Allen 111
  The Philosophy of Composition 111
polyphony 2
popular culture 131–2, 133
Porgy and Bess 44
post-colonialism 107, 119, 122, 127
Powder her Face 94
prima donna 13, 50, 73, 78, 118
primo uomo 13
production book, *see* staging manual
Puccini, Giacomo 9, 32, 38–9, 48, 72, 75, 95–100, 101, 110, 113–14, 120, 123–8, 132
  La bohème 46, 48, 49, 128
  La fanciulla del West 128
  Gianni Schicchi 75
  Madama Butterfly 113–14, 120, 123–8
  Il tabarro 38

Tosca 38, 75, 125
Turandot 38, 39, 110–11, 120
Purcell, Henry 8, 9, 43
  Dido and Aeneas 8
Pushkin, Alexander 34

radio 44, 94
The Rake's Progress 42
Rameau, Jean-Philippe 80
realism 26, 27, 28, 35, 36, 39, 49, 52, 56, 75, 76
recitative 3, 20, 31
Renoir, Pierre-Auguste 102
Renzi, Anna 6
revisions 60–1
Das Rheingold 29
Rhodes, Zandra 63
Ricordi 50, 55, 56, 58, 97, 98
Rigoletto 27, 53, 63–4, 91–5
Rimsky-Korsakov, Nikolai 34
Rinaldo 11
Der Ring des Nibelungen 29, 32, 104
Rinuccini, Ottavio 3
Risorgimento 84, 85, 90
Robinson, Paul 117
Rodgers, Richard 120
  The King and I 120
Romania 34
Rome (ancient civilization) 68, 98
Rome (city) 14, 21, 84, 89, 90, 91, 125
Rossi, Luigi 7
Rossini, Gioachino ix, 21, 22, 23, 26, 28, 72
  Otello 28

Royal Opera House (London)
44, 49, 64, 68, 75
Ruslan and Lyudmila 34
Russia 10, 33–4, 43

Saariaho, Kaija 109
Sacrati, Francesco 7
Sadayakko 125
Said, Edward 122, 128
Salieri, Antonio 16
Salome (Strauss) 40–1, 42, 120
Salome (Wilde) 40
Salzburg 82
San Francisco 48, 133
San Francisco Opera 48
Satyagraha 106
Savoy, House of 83, 89
La Scala (Milan) 87
Scandinavia 34, 43
scenery 4, 6, 24, 35, 51–2, 53,
55, 56, 58, 65, 69, 75,
119, 122, 130
Schikaneder, Emanuel 20
Schoenberg, Arnold 41–2
Erwartung 41–2
Schopenhauer, Arthur 31
Schumann, Robert 102
score 4, 6, 12, 13, 59, 60, 98,
125
Scotland 22, 76, 86, 91, 94,
120
Scott, Sir Walter 22, 94
Sellars, Peter 65
semi opera 8
Senesino (Francesco Bernardi)
13
La serva padrona 16
Sessions, Roger 45

sets, *see* scenery
Shakespeare, William 27–8,
62, 86, 104
Macbeth 27, 86
The Merchant of Venice 104
The Merry Wives of Windsor
28
Othello 27
Sicily 89
Siegfried 29
Simon Boccanegra 28, 61
Singspiel 19–20, 23, 82
Sistine Chapel (Rome) 14
Smart, Mary Ann 87–8
Smetana, Bedřich 34
Smyth, Ethel 43, 109
The Wreckers 109
soccer, *see* football
Soffredini, Alfredo 87
Sonzogno 37
soprano 6, 14, 15, 49, 50
Spain 33, 34, 86, 120, 123
Spohr, Louis 23
St Mark's Cathedral (Venice)
5
staging manual 50, 55, 56, 57,
58
Stanford, Charles Villiers 43
Stiffelio 91
Strauss, Richard 32, 40–1, 49,
120, 126
Ariadne auf Naxos 49
Elektra 40
Salome 40–1, 42, 120
Stravinsky, Igor 38, 42
Oedipus Rex 42
The Rake's Progress 42
Strepponi, Giuseppina 113
Striggio, Alessandro 4

Sue, Eugène 112
  Les Mystères de Paris 112
Suffolk 44
suitcase aria 12
Sullivan, Arthur 9, 34, 120
  Ivanhoe 34
  The Mikado 120, 126
surtitles 59
Swan Lake 56
Switzerland 72
Sydney 57, 71
Sydney Opera House 71
La Sylphide 111
symphony 8, 21, 32, 40, 82,
  107, 108

Il tabarro 38
Tan, Amy 48
  The Bonesetter's Daughter 48
Taruskin, Richard 94
Tate, Nahum 8
Tchaikovsky, Pyotr Ilyich 34,
  105, 109
  Eugene Onegin 34, 109
  Swan Lake 56
Te Kanawa, Kiri 132
Teatro Novissimo (Venice) 51
tenor 8, 14, 15, 65
Terfel, Bryn 132
Thailand 120
Thaïs 33
Theater auf der Wieden
  (Vienna) 20
Théâtre Royal de la Monnaie
  (Brussels) 58
Third Reich 105
Tippett, Michael 44
tone poem 40

Torelli, Giacomo 51
Torrefranca, Fausto 98–9, 101
Tosca 38, 75, 125
Toscanini, Arturo 88
Die Tote Stadt 48
Traetta, Tommaso 10
Tragédie en musique 7, 8
La traviata 27, 36, 48, 53, 72,
  78, 112–13
Tristan und Isolde 30–1
trouser role 118
Il trovatore 27
Turandot 38, 39, 110–11, 120
Turin 21, 83, 84
Turkey 119
Tuscany 97

Upper West Side 71
USA 43, 45, 75, 124, 128, 133

Venice 5, 6, 21, 51, 53, 83,
  84, 92, 93, 119
Verdi, Giuseppe 23, 24–8, 36,
  38, 39, 48, 50, 53, 55–7,
  58, 60, 61, 63–5, 72,
  82–3, 85–9, 91–5, 96, 97,
  98, 105, 112–13, 120,
  122, 133
  Aida 25, 58, 63, 120, 122
  Un ballo in maschera 64
  La battaglia di Legnano 85
  I due Foscari 27
  Ernani 27, 86, 92
  Falstaff 26, 28
  I Lombardi alla prima crociata
    85
  Macbeth 27, 28, 61, 86, 91

Verdi, Giuseppe (*cont.*):
  Nabucco 27, 86–8
  Oberto: conte di San Bonifacio 26
  Otello 27, 28, 57
  Requiem 26
  Rigoletto 27, 53, 63–4, 91–5
  Simon Boccanegra 28, 61
  Stiffelio 91
  La traviata 27, 36, 48, 53, 72, 78, 112–13
  Il trovatore 27
Verga, Giovanni 36
Verismo 35–38, 40, 75
Victor Emanuel, King of Italy 88
Vienna 20, 40, 41, 60, 80, 81
Vietnam War 128
Vinci, Leonardo 10
Virgil 8
  Aeneid 8
Voigt, Deborah 49

Wagner, Richard 11, 23, 24, 28–32, 33, 34, 38, 39, 41, 42, 44, 52–3, 97, 100–6
  Götterdämmerung 29
  Das Judenthum in der Musik 101
  Die Kunst und die Revolution 100
  Die Meistersinger von Nürnberg 29, 103

Parsifal 29, 52, 104
Das Rheingold 29
Der Ring des Nibelungen 29, 32, 104
Siegfried 29
Tristan und Isolde 30–1
Die Walküre 29
Wagner, Wieland 53
Die Walküre 29
Wallace, Stewart 48
  The Bonesetter's Daughter 48
Walton, William 44
Weber, Carl Maria von 23
  Der Freischütz 23
Weill, Kurt 45
Weir, Judith 109
Wesendonck, Mathilde 31
Wilde, Oscar 40
  Salome 40
Wilson, Robert 58
Wlaschin, Ken 74
World Cup 38, 132
Wozzeck 42
The Wreckers 109

Yugoslavia 34

Die Zauberflöte, see The Magic Flute
Zeffirelli, Franco 75, 78
Zeno, Apostolo 10
Zurich 72

A Beginner's Guide to Classical Music

9781851686872
£9.99/ $14.95

What does classical music
mean to the Western World?
How has it transformed over
the centuries? With such a rich
tradition, what relevance does
it have today? Julian Johnson
inspires readers to explore the
field, and examines how music is
related to some of the big ideas
of Western experience including
spirituality, emotion, the weight
of history, and self identity.

"Johnson combines boundless enthusiasm for the subject
with extensive knowledge and manages to convey a decent
quantity of the latter in economical and effortless fashion."
Classical Music

JULIAN JOHNSON is currently Professor of Music
at Royal Holloway, University of London. He is also a
composer and public speaker on musicology, championing
the relevance of classical music to the general public.

Browse further titles at
www.oneworld-publications.com

A Beginner's Guide to The French Revolution

9781851686933
£9.99/ $14.95

Blending narrative with analysis, Peter Davies explores a time of obscene opulence, mass starvation, and ground-breaking ideals; where the streets of Paris ran red with blood, and the numbers requiring execution precipitated the invention of the guillotine.

Davies brings the subject up to date by considering the legacy of the revolution and how it continues to resonate in today's France.

PETER DAVIES is senior lecturer in History at the University of Huddersfield. His previous books include 'The Debate about the French Revolution' and 'The Extreme Right in France: From de Maistre to Le Pen'. He has also written about fascism, the far right, small-group teaching and learning, and the social history of cricket.